# Dena's Fuel for Fitness:

## Moving from Animal-based Grub to Plant-based Fuel

### "pleas'n every vegan"

## Dena Mangiamele

### DVM, MPVM, MFS
### Vegan Tri-athlete

## Disclaimer:

Although every effort has been made to ensure that the contents of this book are accurate, it must not be treated as a substitute for medical advice. Always seek the advice of your physician or other qualified health provider with any questions you may have regarding a medical condition. The author cannot be held responsible for any loss or claim arising out of use, or misuse, of the suggestions made.

## Statements:

## Credits:

- Alyssa Rachel | Photographer, Food Stylist: www.alyssarachel.net

Dena's Skincare/Makeup all vegan:
- BOOM by Cindy Joseph: www.boombycindyjoseph.com
- India Dunn, HairDresser, SalonIndia, Creative Compassionate Coaching: www.indiadunn.com
- Sally B's Skin Yummies (www.sallybskinyummies.com),
- thrive causemetics (www.thrivecausemetics.com),
- 100% Pure (www.100percentpure.com)

## Speaker/Author Contact Information:

Dr. Dena Mangiamele is author of the Amazon Best Selling Book, *Stray: A Shelter Veterinarian's Reflection on Triumph and Tragedy.* She's also a vegan tri-athlete. If you want a speaker for an upcoming event, Dr. Dena provides lectures, writes editorials/blogs, and does book signings.

- www.doctordena.com
- contact@doctordena.com

## Table of Contents

# Introduction

Organization is the key to many of life's challenges, including successful lifestyle changes such as conversion to healthy plant-based eating habits. If you can master the easy organizational skills I outline in this book, you can become and maintain a healthier you, which will promote a higher quality of your life permanently.

## What is a plant-based diet?

There are varying degrees of what are considered to be vegetarian-based diets. A vegetarian diet is one that is based on a minimal consumption of meat, fish or poultry. There are various labels used to describe these, depending on how much animal-based protein is included in the diet. You have:

- lacto-ovo vegetarian which allows for consumption of eggs and dairy products
- lacto-vegetarian which includes dairy products, but not eggs
- The term plant-based diet is interchanged with the word vegan. This diet does not include the consumption of any animal products and is based on eating foods in as close to its whole, unadulterated state as possible.

As you will find as you read on in this book, there are many health and disease prevention benefits attributed to this diet and lifestyle that promote longevity.

## How do you start to transition to a plant-based diet?

First step is to change your mindset. How you feed your body must take top priority in your life until you can go on plant-based auto-pilot. You will need to change your taste buds from processed, high sugar, low nutrient foods to nutrient dense whole foods. It won't happen overnight so be patient with your body during the adjustment. It is also important to acknowledge that when you embrace a plant-based diet many of the foods are low in calories which actually requires you to eat more of these foods, not less, in order to achieve your daily intake of healthy nutrients. You should never feel deprived when eating a plant-based diet.

You will know when you have officially crossed into the plant-based lifestyle when you recognize improved energy levels, digestion, and you will probably lose weight. Other positive signs include clear skin and healthy hair. From an emotional level you will have an increased awareness of your body and truly appreciate caring for it daily – with every meal you will be confident that you are in control of your body and your longevity.

The physical adjustments you will need to make to embrace this lifestyle include removing all processed foods, those heavy with preservatives/food additives, and high in sugar and replacing them with primarily whole foods. You will have greater success with your transition if you do not smoke, do not use recreational drugs, and do not drink alcohol. Indulging in these activities causes your body to devote energy and detoxification actions to clear their side effects rather than being one hundred percent readily available to confront viruses, cancer, and/or auto-immune issues.

## Why are processed foods harmful to your body?

Through the act of processing a food, it loses many essential nutrients and contains additives that are difficult for your body to process or remove. If your diet consists primarily of refined processed foods over time your body can become depleted in key nutrients while additives can accumulate which negatively affects your health and longevity.

## Why are preservatives or food additives harmful to your body?

Preservatives are added to foods to maintain freshness, maintain nutritional status, and to improve the taste, texture and appearance (color additives) of a food product. Approval of preservatives by the Food & Drug Administration (FDA) is a complicated process with some substances designated as "generally accepted as safe" (GRAS) without testing and often the food industry makes the decision if a substance is GRAS. There are also some approved substances that are linked to cancer (e.g., BHA, artificial sweeteners like aspartame). Their approval is based on small dosage consumption, but consideration for multiple preservatives in products (additive effects) and frequency of consumption of products with food additives (dose-related effects) has not been accurately evaluated. Prolonged ingestion of additives could accumulate in your body and increase negative health risks, including cancer.

### Why are foods high in sugar harmful to your body?

Added sugars like sucrose and high fructose corn syrup contain a lot of calories without any essential nutrients (empty calories). When you eat sugar, it is broken down in the G.I. tract into glucose and fructose. When there is too much glucose in the blood, it can cause insulin resistance, negatively affecting metabolism, obesity, cardiovascular disease, and Type II diabetes. The liver metabolizes fructose and if eaten in small amounts (e.g., from fruit) it can be turned into glycogen and stored in the liver until we need the energy source. The problem comes in when you consume large amounts of sugar and the liver has maximized its storage capacity of glycogen so fructose in the liver is converted into fat. Some of this fat can get lodged in the liver resulting in non-alcoholic fatty liver disease. Fructose also doesn't lower the hunger hormone ghrelin as much as glucose, resulting in an increased calorie intake. High sugar intake can increase your cancer risk due to continual increased insulin levels and the inability to adequately regulate cell growth and multiplication. Also, metabolic problems associated with high sugar intake increase your risk for heart disease, and increases inflammation throughout the body which contributes to the propagation of cancer. The reason sugar is addictive is that it causes a release of dopamine in the reward center of the brain.

### Nutrition Basics

The recommended distribution of protein, fat, and carbohydrate in the overall diet is:

- **Protein 10-15%**
- **Fat 15-30%**
- **Carbohydrate 55-75%**

### What do I need to know about proteins?

Proteins (aka, the building blocks of life) are made up of different amino acids linked together. The function of protein in our body is to promote cell growth and repair. Proteins digest slower than carbohydrates which help you feel fuller longer which means you probably will consume fewer calories when eating protein-rich foods.

The U.S. Recommended Dietary Allowance (RDA) for adult protein intake is 0.8g/kg of body weight. For people eating a plant-based diet there are foods that are highly digestible (e.g., tofu, lentils, refined grains) and other protein sources that are less digestible. To compensate for this, the recommended adult protein intake on a plant-based diet has been adjusted to 0.9g/kg body weight (average range 45-70g/day). On average you will need about 3 to 4 grams of protein for every 100 calories you consume.

To calculate your daily recommended protein intake of 0.9g/kg of weight use the following formula:

1. **First convert weight in pounds to weight in kg. Take your weight in pounds and divide by 2.2 lb/kg = weight in kg.**
2. **Take weight in kg and multiply by 0.9 = your recommended daily protein intake**

In order to see how easily you can attain your daily protein requirement on a plant-based diet, here are some examples of plant-based foods from the recipe section of the book and their grams of protein per serving:

**Soy beans 1 cup = 28.6 grams of protein**

**Firm Tofu ½ cup = 20 grams of protein**

**Lentils 1 cup = 18 grams protein**

**Tempeh ½ cup = 15.8 grams of protein**

**Beans 1 cup (pinto, garbanzo, kidney) =**
**14.0-15.4 grams of protein**

**Sesame Tahini 3 tbsp = 8.1 grams of protein**

**Sunflower seeds/Pumpkin seeds ¼ cup =**
**8.0-8.5 grams of protein**

**Kale 1 cup = 2.2 grams of protein**

## What do I need to know about carbohydrates?

Carbohydrates are made by plants and are not found in animal products. Glucose, considered a simple carbohydrate is created through photosynthesis. Plants make other sugars by rearranging the sugar, glucose. Carbohydrates are categorized based on the units of sugar that are linked together (mono-, di-, polysaccharides). Fiber falls in the category of polysaccharides that cannot be completely digested. The standard Western diet is generally deficient in fiber. When you eat a balanced plant-based diet you will be consuming the recommended 27-40 grams of fiber per day (vegans on average consume 40-50 grams of fiber per day). Some of the positive aspects of fiber intake include reducing total and LDL cholesterol (preventing heart disease), protection against colorectal, pancreatic and breast cancer, decreases hemorrhoids, protects against gallstones and may protect against inflammatory bowel diseases.

Carbohydrates provide the major energy supply for the body in the most efficient and safest manner, as compared with other energy sources like protein and fat. The energy value of carbohydrates ranges from 2kcal/g – 4kcal/g dependent on the sources being completely digestible or those not digested at all (e.g., fiber).

Other functions of carbohydrates from foods include controlling blood sugar, cholesterol, and triglyceride levels. Within the digestive tract, carbohydrates help prevent constipation and support bacterial flora in the large bowel.

The Food and Agriculture Organization (FAO) of the United Nations and the World Health Organization (WHO) recommend the healthy/average diet consists of 55% - 75% of calories from a variety of whole food, carbohydrate sources (legumes, whole grains, vegetables, fruits, nuts, and seeds). When the percentage falls below 55% of whole food energy sources, protein and fat intake pick up the slack which increases the risk of chronic diseases.

## What do I need to know about fats?

Most diets demonize fat despite the fact that it is an essential part of a healthy lifestyle. Disease risk is correlated based on the types of fat rather than the amount of fat in your diet. If fat sources are plant-based (see below), you can eat a higher proportion of fat in your total caloric intake and still maintain excellent health. But if your fat intake comes from animal sources and processed foods, even a small to moderate amount of fat in your total caloric intake over time, can result in chronic disease. Fats help with the absorption of fat soluble vitamins (A, D, E, K). Fatty acids are the basic component of fats and oils. They are essential to cell membranes, anti-inflammatory properties, and regulating cholesterol. Let's get a simple review of fat jargon and scientific information on which types are beneficial to your health.

**Fatty acid catagories—saturated and unsaturated (2 types):**

- **Saturated fatty acids (SFA) = bad fats**, hard at room temperature, main source is animal products, linked to increases in blood cholesterol, heart disease, and some forms of cancer. Most higher-fat plant foods contain minimal saturated fat while they are in high concentration in animal products and tropical oils (except coconut oil which provides health benefits - more on this later). Examples of SFAs can be found in: butter, cream, cakes, pastries, hard cheese, hydrogenated fat (used in production of biscuits and pastries).

- **Monounsaturated fatty acids (MUFA) = neutral to slightly beneficial effect on health**, liquid at room temperature, and semi-solid when refrigerated, can protect against chronic diseases, especially heart disease.

1. Slightly increases "good" (HDL) cholesterol levels and improves blood sugar control in people with diabetes.
2. Examples of foods containing MUFAs are avocados, olive oil, olives, and most nuts (see next page).

- **Trans fatty acids = a bad type of MUFA,** more damaging than any other type of fat. Fats containing trans fatty acids were developed through food processing to improve shelf life and increase the melting point of fats so they could be used for deep frying (e.g., for fast food production) without risking rancidity of the fat at high temperatures. 90% of consumption from processed and fried foods, 10% of consumption from meat and dairy products. Examples of foods high in trans fatty acids are: margarine, shortening, crackers, cookies, chips, snack foods, deep fried foods.

- **Polyunsaturated fatty acids (PUFA) = favorable effect on health,** liquid at room temperature and when refrigerated, they include two essential (meaning they are required in the diet) fatty acids (EFA) classified in the omega family.

  1. **omega-3 fatty acids = alpha linolenic acid (ALA).** More favorable health benefits than omega-6 fatty acids. They have been increasingly more difficult to obtain in the standard diet since they are a delicate substance that is easily broken down through the current level of food processing. Examples: flax oil, hemp, ground flax, and chia seeds, walnuts, marine algae, leafy greens, broccoli, cabbage.

  2. **omega-6 fatty acids = linoleic acid (LA).** They have become more prevalent in the standard diet when saturated fat was replaced by vegetable oils. Examples: safflower oil, corn oil, pumpkin and sesame seeds, soybeans, walnuts, and grains.

  3. The intake of omegas must be properly balanced and may prevent and control a number of inflammatory conditions such as heart disease and arthritis. The ideal ratio of LA: ALA is 3:1. The standard diet provides as much as 20 times as much of LA as ALA.

**Cholesterol** is a waxy fat-like substance, the most common steroid found in the body and most of it is made by the liver (and also cleared from the body by the liver) and intestines. Only about 20% of cholesterol in our body comes from foods we eat, especially animal products (eggs, organ meats, shellfish). Since cholesterol is a fat it needs to be packaged with a protein-covered particle becoming a **lipoprotein (lipid plus protein)** in order to mix easily with blood so it can be transported throughout the body.

**There are five main types of lipoproteins** but the two that get the most attention are:

- **High density lipoprotein (HDL, high proportion of protein to fat in the lipoprotein package)** – the protective/good form of cholesterol which takes excess cholesterol from circulation and artery walls and returns it to the liver for removal. This is the lipoprotein you want more of in your body.

- **Low density lipoprotein (LDL, low proportion of protein to fat in the lipoprotein package)** – the harmful form of cholesterol because it delivers cholesterol to tissues and associated with artery-clogging plaque and increased risk of cardiovascular disease.

## What do I need to know about fiber?

Fiber is an important component of a healthy diet. Regular, unstrained bowel movements are an indicator of digestive health. The gut is not only the location of nutrient absorption but also promotes an effective immune system. High fiber diets have also been shown to be associated with better blood sugar control and with much better weight control. People should consume between 21 and 38g of fiber per day, depending on age and sex according to the National Academy of Sciences. The average American consumes around 11g of fiber daily. Keep an eye out for high fiber foods identified in Step Two: List of whole foods recommended for the four-month conversion to a plant-based lifestyle.

Example of fiber content in plant-based foods in descending order:

Raspberries > apples and pears > buckwheat groats > oranges > oatmeal > blueberries > strawberries > brown rice

## Next Steps

With that background on the health risks associated with a Western diet and a foundation in basic nutrition, here are the easy steps outlined in the remainder of the book that will be the keys to your success in converting to a plant-based life style.

- **Step One: Learn the Benefits**
- **Step Two: The Secret to Healthy Living is Getting Organized; organize your kitchen, organize your life**
- **Step Three: Recommended Foods for the Four-Month Plant-Based Conversion**
- **Step Four: Library of Recipes for the Four Month Plant-Based Conversion**
- **Step Five: Month One Meal Plan for the Plant-Based Conversion**
- **Step Six:  How to Develop Weekly Shopping Lists that Match the Weekly Menu**
- **Step Seven: Guidelines for Matching Food Prep with the Weekly Meal Plan**

## Step One: Learn the Benefits

Once I made the commitment to go plant-based, I wasted years stumbling around trying to organize nutrition information on plant-based foods, figuring out what equipment and techniques I needed to efficiently and safely prep whole foods, and learning how to plan nutritionally balanced meals. There are so many things I wish I knew when I started my journey. This book is dedicated to giving you everything you need to know in one place to jump start your plant-based lifestyle.

I began my nutrition journey about 20 years ago as a triathlete when I realized, how I fueled my body directly affected my athletic and day-to day performance and energy levels. Even though fitness is not directly addressed in this book, physical activity and regular workouts at whatever level you are comfortable will also greatly contribute to your quality of life and longevity.

I began my conversion to becoming vegetarian slowly. During that time period I lost both of my parents to cancer and began researching preventive measures for chronic diseases. As I spent more time separating fad dietary changes from scientific research on cause and effect dietary influences on health, I was amazed at how much I didn't know about the value of paying attention to how we fuel our bodies. As a medical professional, I analyzed the data and was convinced the plant-based, vegan lifestyle was the right choice for me. I took the time to study up on basic nutrition, identify plant-based foods that delivered all of the nutrients I needed, and started a recipe library to ensure I was staying current on food trends and pairings.

Twenty years later, not only am I a real-life vegan athlete/enthusiast, but I also created and operated a vegan/raw snack business with products sold in gourmet markets such as Whole Foods in five states and large on-line grocers such as Thrive Market serving healthy people around the country. While promoting my products in stores around the country I spent a lot of time talking to everyday people with varying backgrounds, food preferences, and lifestyles. One thing they all had in common was that they wanted to live their healthiest life and after sampling my healthy snacks they were amazed vegan food could taste so good! I knew at that point that this was a "messaging" issue and if I could provide the resources for people to convert from the Western diet to a plant-based diet in a simple manual that provided the basic information to promote the health and longevity for them and their loved ones that took me years to accumulate, they would be more interested in becoming plant-based.

Here my friends, is your resource guide to get you started in this important journey. As you embrace the plant-based lifestyle remember you are also contributing to a better environment and taking a stand against animal cruelty. Don't miss out on all the benefits a plant-based lifestyle has to offer. You must take the first step by committing to make a change in the manner in which you fuel your body. What you do today determines how your body supports and protects you for the rest of your life.

Cheers to a healthier, longer, high quality plant-based life! — **Dr. Dena**

## Step Two: Organize Your Kitchen

**The secret to healthy living is getting organized—organize your kitchen, organize your life...**

As with any task or project, identifying and properly using the correct equipment not only makes the job easier and safer but it also helps to expedite the task. Part of the successful strategy of being plant-based is becoming organized in your kitchen. As you become familiar with and learn how to effectively use the equipment in your kitchen, it will enhance your cooking and meal preparation skills and raise your comfort level one step closer to fully embracing the plant-based lifestyle.

This section identifies, by name and photo, the equipment, utensils, and containers you will need to be fully operational in the kitchen on Day One of your transformation to plant-based living. While reviewing the entire list, you may discover many of the items you already have in your kitchen. If some of your current equipment (e.g., blender and food processor) are older models, it would be valuable to compare their power and food capacity to newer models. If they don't measure up, I strongly suggest you purchase a new model to ensure the food you are preparing reaches the desired texture and consistency expected from each recipe.

At the end of this section I have created a table that lists the items and their range of cost so you can plan what level of investment you will need to complete your kitchen set-up, which is the first organizational step in becoming plant-based. Remember that these pieces of equipment will serve you well for many, many years and will be used repeatedly each week as you move into a plant-based diet.

### High-End Equipment

**Blender –** The top kitchen tool is a high-speed blender. Compared to other blenders, these machines dramatically decrease blending time while producing the best texture to the finished product. You will use the blender for smoothies, salad dressings, dips, soups, and nanacream (banana based ice cream). The high-speed blenders below were identified by Bestproducts.com Best Smoothie Blenders 2018.

**Food Processor –** Used for chopping, slicing, dicing, mincing, shredding mixing, blending, raw desserts/pie crusts. It may seem like you can use a blender for the same tasks that can be completed with a food processor. If the recipe requires moisture (e.g., water, nut milk, juice) it can be more efficiently handled with a blender. If your recipe requires a thicker mixture (raw energy bars) or a task doesn't include moisture (chopping fruit/vegetables), you will need to use a food processor. Also, processors have different attachments to customize slicing thickness and patterns which enhance the chef's creativity and dish presentation. The food processors below were identified by Bestreviews.com, Best Food Processors 2018.

Vitamix Blender

Ninja Professional Blender

Hamilton Beach Power Elite Blender

Breville Food Processor

Cuisinart Food Processor

Hamilton Beach Food Processor

# 8 — Organize Your Kitchen

## Other Equipment, Utensils, Bowls and Containers:

**Spiralizer**

**Box Grater**

**Microplane —citrus zest**

**Salad Spinner**

**Colander**

**Citrus Juicer**

**Frying Pans—Eco Pans**

**Cookware**

**Steamer**

**Cutting Boards**

**Measuring Cups/Spoons**

**Can Opener**

**Knives (paring, wide-blade, serrated...)**

**Ladle**

**Wooden Spoons & Spatula**

**Large Mixing Spoons & Large Slotted Spoon**

**Spatula**

**Mixing Bowls (stainless steel)**

**Mason Jars & Lids (all sizes)**

**Cheese Cloth or Milk Bag**

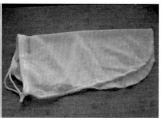
**Salad Bowl**

**Glass Food Storage Containers (all sizes)**

## Price Range Chart for Plant-Based Kitchen Equipment, Utensils, Bowls and Containers

This chart provides basic guidelines for suggested product manufacturers and price ranges. Make sure you complete your own Internet search on products (especially high-end equipment) prior to purchase to ensure they meet your preferences.

| EQUIPMENT | Models/Sizes | PRICE RANGE |
|---|---|---|
| Blender | Vitamix<br>Ninja Professional<br>Hamilton Beach Power Elite | $299.00-399.00<br>$90.00<br>$36.00 |
| Food Processor | Breville<br>Cuisinart 14 -cup<br>Hamilton Beach – 10 cup | $385.00<br>$258.00<br>$60.00 |
| Steamer | Oster 5-Quart to Viante Intellisteam | $25.00-250.00 |
| Spiralizer | Multiple blades | $27.00-40.00 |
| Box Grater | 4-sided, 6-sided graters | $6.99-15.00 |
| Salad spinner | | $15.00-24.99 |
| Microplane | | $13.00-20.99 |
| Colander (stainless steel) | 1.5-quart, 3-quart, 5-quart; or all 3 | $4.99-24.99 |
| Citrus Juicer | Hand-held to electric | $15.99-39.99 |
| Frying pans | Eco pans – ceramic (non-stick surface)<br>Small, medium, large; 3 to 12 pc sets | $15.00-149.99 |
| Cookware | Eco friendly – GreenPan, Cuisinart  10-pc and 12-pc sets<br>1 qt saucepan w/lid | $149.99 - 199.00<br><br>$15.99-24.95 |
| Cutting boards (eco friendly) | Bamboo, Epicurean | $14.99-21.99 |
| Measuring cups, stainless (set)<br>Measuring spoons, stainless | | $19.99-22.99<br>$12.99-17.85 |
| Can opener | Hand-held to Electric | $7.99-26.95 |
| Cheese Cloth/Milk Bag | | $3.00-5.99 |
| UTENSILS | | |
| Knives | Paring<br>Serrated<br>Wide blade 8-10 inch | $18.00<br>$14.00-32.00<br>$28.00-150.00 |
| Large mixing spoons | Wooden, silicone | $5.99-8.49 |
| Large slotted spoon | Wooden, silicone | $6.50-8.95 |
| Ladle | Stainless steel | $11.00-14.00 |
| Spatula | Stainless steel, silicone | $5.80-10.95 |
| BOWLS/CONTAINERS | | |
| Mixing bowls (stainless steel) | Set of four to five with lids | $27.99-44.95 |
| Glass food storage containers* | 3-6 pack various sizes with lids | $22.49-25.00 |
| Salad Bowl | Glass, stainless, wooden | $19.99-25.00 |
| Mason jars with lids | Bell Mason Jars with lids, 12-pack 8 oz, 12 oz, 16 oz | $6.00-$8.40-$11.16 |

Regarding the table above, please note that glass containers can be used for warm/hot food storage, in contrast to plastic containers that can potentially leach harmful chemicals (BPA, or bisphenol-A – used to harden plastics) from container to food after repeated use/heating in the microwave. This leaching is dangerous to your health (possible hormone disruption and concerns for children's health). Besides glass containers, other safe materials include: ceramic, stainless steel, stoneware, and silicone. Glass Mason Jars also make great food storage containers in the pantry for nuts, seeds, and dried fruits.

As you become more comfortable with the plant-based lifestyle and expand your recipe files beyond the four-month transformation proposed in this book, you may want to consider adding other pieces of equipment to your kitchen:

- Centrifugal Juice Extractor
- Masticating Juicer
- Dehydrator
- Sprouters/Seed Sprouting Jars

**Equipment Resource Guide**

| Company | Website |
| --- | --- |
| Vitamix | www.vitamix.com |
| Breville | www.breville.com |
| Hamilton Beach | www.hamiltonbeach.com |
| Ninja | www.ninjakitchen.com |
| Cuisinart | www.cuisinart.com |
| Oster | www.oster.com |
| Viante Intellisteam | www.vianteusa.com |
| Amazon | www.amazon.com |

## Step Three: Recommended Foods for the Four-Month Plant-Based Conversion

The foods on the pantry list that follows are the minimum items you will need in order to make all of the plant-based recipes in this book. That doesn't mean you can't add other fruits and vegetables, many of which you can snack on raw or substitute in our versatile recipes. Also, as you are transitioning to a plant-based diet, you could start with one meal a day (breakfast, lunch, or dinner) and stock your pantry for those recipes only. As you expand your transition, you will be adding the other items to your pantry until, eventually, you will have a fully stocked, healthy pantry from which you can create all of the recipes provided in this book and beyond.

One of the most common discussions among plant-based enthusiasts regarding which foods should we be putting into our bodies is whether or not each item must be organic. Everyone needs to decide for themselves if they want all organic (no exceptions) or if some conventional foods can be consumed along with organic items. Here are some facts to consider about whole foods and pesticide contamination to help guide you with your grocery shopping.

What does organic mean and which foods should you purchase organic?

The definition of organic means no synthetic fertilizers, pesticides, sewage sludge and organic farmers and production plants must not use irradiation or any genetic engineering. Keep in mind there are different levels of organic (based on the percentage of the product's ingredients that are organic).

Organic produce has a 30 percent lower risk of pesticide contamination than conventional fruits and vegetables. Be aware that organic foods are not necessarily 100 percent free of pesticides. Based on the annual Environmental Working Group (EWG) listing here is your guide for which foods you should try to buy organic because the conventional variety test results recorded heavy contamination with pesticides:

**Strawberries, apples, grapes, nectarines, peaches, celery, cherries, spinach, tomatoes, sweet bell peppers, cherry tomatoes, cucumbers, leafy greens**

Fruits and vegetables with thick skins, those you peel prior to eating, and those that have lower pesticide levels because they don't attract as many harmful insects don't have to necessarily be purchased as organic. Here is the list of foods (some can be identified by their thick skin or outer layer) that you don't have to buy organic:

**Avocados, bananas, pineapple, mangoes, papayas, grapefruit, cantaloupe, cauliflower, asparagus, eggplant, onions, kiwi, cabbage, sweet potatoes, sweet corn**

Part of the plant-based lifestyle is not only to eat plants, but to be responsible in reducing or eliminating food waste and ensuring that every dollar you spend on food is well spent. This is another reason why meal planning is also important so you can choose dishes that share many of the same ingredients, which decreases the potential of food spoilage by the end of the week. As you will see in the recipe section, many snacks, dressings, soups, and meals can be double batched and extra portions frozen for consumption up to two weeks later. This will minimize any waste due to spoilage and provide you with the greatest, healthiest value for every dollar you spend on whole ingredients.

As for your weekly supply of fresh "greens", this is where my Greens and Fruit breakfast comes in handy to decrease waste since it adds another serving of greens to your daily intake as well as boosts your nutritional profile. Smoothies also present a great opportunity to customize the drink to whatever remaining ingredients you have in the refrigerator or in the fruit bowl – be creative.

So that you can easily become familiar with the whole foods you will be purchasing from the market, you will find in this section fourteen **food charts** that identify:

1. Food / product categories: Fruits, Dried Fruit, Greens, Vegetables, Legumes/Soy, Seeds, Nuts, Spices/Herbs, Oils, Condiments, Algae/Seaweed, Miscellaneous Products, Baking Supplies, and Plant-Based Protein Powders

2. The best type of kitchen storage for each food / product

3. Which foods to buy organic

4. Nutritional profile (top nutrients found in each food). Use the daily recommended intakes for common nutrients listed below when comparing individual food values:

   a. Recommended calcium intake 1000-1200mg

   b. Recommended Iron intake 14.4-32.4 mg (women). Absorb more Iron by eating calcium-rich foods at the same time.

   c. Recommended protein intake 0.9g/kg body weight (average range 45-70g/day)

   d. Recommended carbohydrate intake 27-40 grams of fiber per day, diet consists of 55% - 75% of calories from a variety of whole food, carbohydrate sources.

   e. Recommended fat intake 15-30% of daily diet

   f. Recommended fiber intake 21 and 38g of fiber per day

Some of the foods/products listed in the charts may not be common to everyone, so there is a section at the end of Step Three that provides additional information on these select items including: enhanced description of the food/product, its common use in cooking/dish preparation, and nutritional benefits.

**Definitions for Nutritional Information Commonly Used in the Food Charts:**

**Antioxidants:** fight off the destructive effects of oxidation to cells and DNA caused by harmful free radicals by neutralizing and removing the free radicals from the bloodstream. This damage can influence the development of atherosclerosis (blood vessel disease), cancer, eye issues, and immune system problems. Different antioxidants interact with different parts of the body: for example, flavonoids benefit heart health while carotenoids benefit eye health.

**There are three main types of antioxidants:**

1.  **Enzymes** – antioxidant enzymes are synthesized in the body and made from the protein and minerals we eat.

2.  **Vitamins** – antioxidant vitamins must be supplemented and include:

    a.  **Vitamin A – fat soluble,** (alpha and beta-carotene can be metabolized to Vitamin A), common in vegetables and fruit

    b.  **Vitamin B – water soluble,** eight vitamins, common in grains and legumes (except B12). Thiamine (B1), Riboflavin (B2), Niacin (B3), Pantothenic Acid (B5), Pyridoxine (B6), Biotin (B7), Folate (B9 - folic acid is the synthetic form of folate found in supplements and added to processed foods), and cyanocobalamin (B12)

    c.  **Vitamin C - water soluble,** common in vegetables and fruit

    d.  **Vitamin D - fat soluble,** plant sourced vitamin supplement or product fortification is listed as: ergosterol or ergocalciferol. Our bodies make Vitamin D when exposed to sunlight, a compound in the oil glands of our skin is transformed to a pre-vitamin D form, and in further processes converted to the active form of Vitamin D.

    e.  **Vitamin E - fat soluble,** common in oils of nuts and seeds

    f.  **Vitamin K - fat soluble,** common in the oils of leafy greens.

3.  **Phytochemicals/Phytonutrients -** Chemicals/nutrients produced by plants to protect themselves, and when we ingest these plants, the phytochemicals have antioxidant properties within our bodies.

**Phytonutrients with Antioxidant Activity:**

1.  **Polyphenols** (phenolics) are micronutrients with antioxidant properties, there are over 8,000 identified polyphenols found in foods. The richest food sources of polyphenols include: raw fruits (especially berries) and vegetables, seeds, spices/herbs. Since polyphenols are fat soluble, eating them with fats optimizes their absorption making them more bioavailable. Multiple types of phenols can be found in a fruit or vegetable. Fruits with the highest concentration of polyphenols include strawberries and grapes. Vegetables with the highest concentration of polyphenols include artichokes, parsley, and brussel sprouts. Melons and avocados have the lowest concentrations of polyphenols. Polyphenols can be broken down into four categories:

    a.  **Flavonoids (over 4,000)** – are color producing compounds and also play a protective role (biological effects) for the plant against attacks by insects or microbes such as bacteria. When we consume flavonoids through plants, we receive numerous health benefits such as antioxidant and anti-inflammatory protections resulting in a reduced risk of certain cancers, heart disease, and age-related degenerative diseases. Flavonoids can be found in fruits, vegetables, legumes, green tea, chocolate, and red wine.

        *   **Flavones** – produce the color yellow
        *   **Flavonols** – produce the color yellow and are the most common of all categories of flavonoids. They are abundant in the following foods: onions, leeks, broccoli, kale, berries (especially blueberries). The two most common flavonols based on biologic effects (not necessarily yellow in color) are: Quercetin (anti-cancer and anti-inflammatory activity) found in onions, asparagus, lettuce, berries, and cocoa; kaempferol found in spinach, kale, and some spices
        *   **Flavanones** – in citrus
        *   **Isoflavones** - major flavonoid found in legumes, particularly soybeans
        *   **Anthocyanins** – are water soluble pigments responsible for most red,

blue, and purple colors in higher plants. Biological effects: when consumed, provide antioxidant benefits and have been well established to provide cardiovascular support. Foods containing anthocyanins include: berries, cherries, eggplant.

b. **Lignans** – found in seeds (highest in flax seeds, sesame, poppy), legumes, grains (oat bran), fruits (apricots, strawberries) algae, and certain vegetables (kale, broccoli). Lignans are associated with preventing hormone-related cancers because of their estrogen-like (mimicking) activity

c. **Phenolic acids** – found in tea, cinnamon, blueberries, kiwi, plums, apples, cherries, and coffee. One example is **Ellagic Acid (tannin)**: a polyphenol compound present in fruits, nuts, and seeds including pomegranates, blackberries, raspberries, strawberries, cranberries, walnuts, and almonds. Associated with antioxidant, anti-inflammatory, and anticarcinogenic activities, in laboratory models inhibits the growth of tumors caused by certain carcinogens.

d. **Stilbenes** – found in red wine (resveratrol) and peanuts. **Resveratrol** is a phytonutrient, a phytoalexin compound found in grapes, blueberries, cranberries, and cocoa. It's associated with a reduced risk of cardiovascular disease and cancer through antioxidant and anti-inflammatory activities, it promotes anti-aging, and it may help slow cognitive decline.

2. **Carotenoids** – are pigment molecules, but not responsible for the major pigment in plants. Generally, bright red, yellow and orange colors are often caused by carotenoids either by themselves or in combination with flavonoids. Some well-known carotenoids include: **carotenes** (alpha, beta) = orange in carrots, cantaloupe, mangoes, papaya, sweet potatoes, pumpkin; **lycopene** = red in tomatoes, watermelon, papaya, red bell peppers); **chlorophyll** is the pigment in green vegetables.

More than 750 different carotenoids can be found in the cells of plants. When we consume carotenoids through plants, we receive numerous health benefits including antioxidant benefits that combat cellular damage, support cardiovascular health, and protect vision. For example, the most common carotenoids include carotenes (alpha, beta) that protect against cellular damage as Vitamin A (retinol) precursors, while zeaxanthin and lutein are not Vitamin A precursors but are selectively taken up by the eye (the only carotenoids found in the retina) where they help maintain vision and provide protection against macular degeneration. Carotenoids need to be consumed with a fat in order for the body to absorb them.

3. **Allyl sulfides** found in garlic and onions which may trigger and improve detoxification enzyme levels to inactivate carcinogens

4. **Isothiocyanates** – the breakdown of glucosinolates into sulfur-containing compounds of this group such as sulforaphane and indoles (indole-3-carbinol). They are found in cruciferous vegetables (broccoli, cabbage, Brussel sprouts, kale, watercress), mustard, and papaya seeds, and their health benefits include: antioxidant, anti-inflammatory, neutralizing carcinogens, and they stimulate the release of other substances that fight cancer cells.

### Other nutrition terms and definitions:

**Fructoogliosaccharides (FOS):** food for good bacteria/probiotics in your gut

**Oxygen Radical Absorbance Capacity (ORAC):** testing procedure used by the USDA to determine the antioxidant and phytochemical power of plant food

**Glycemic Index:** Measures how much a given food raises blood sugar

**Glycemic Load:** Measure of a food's effect on blood sugar that takes into account portion size

# 14 — Recommended Foods

## FRUIT FOOD CHART

| FRUIT | KITCHEN STORAGE | NUTRITIONAL PROFILE |
|---|---|---|
| Apples – buy organic<br><br>High antioxidant activity in apple peels | Countertop | Quercetin (flavonoid) may help prevent cancer cell replication and reduce risk of lung cancer, second highest antioxidant activity in fruit, pectin (soluble fiber) lowers LDL and helps regulate blood sugar, boron for bone building |
| Bananas<br>Inner peel rich in nutrients | Countertop/Frozen | Fiber, potassium, FOS, glycemic load is low to medium (sugar) |
| Oranges/Tangerines<br>Many nutrients found in the pulp and peel, more benefits eating the whole fruit versus juicing | Countertop | Vit C, phytochemicals (including anti-cancer limonoids) and flavonoids (hesperidin which strengthens capillaries, anti-inflammatory, anti-cancer), fiber |
| Lemons | Countertop | Vit C, antioxidant, anti-inflammatory, anti-cancer limeonene (in the peel) |
| Limes | Countertop | Vit C, anti-cancer limeonene (in the peel) |
| Blueberries – buy organic | Refrigerate | Anti-oxidant (one of highest ORAC), anti-inflammatory, polyphenols (provide memory support) |
| Strawberries – buy organic | Refrigerate | Ellagic Acid in laboratory models inhibit certain tumor growth, antioxidants, some anthocyanin activity that inhibits the enzyme signaling pain and inflammation with arthritis, fiber, calcium, magnesium, phosphorus, potassium, Vit C |
| Raspberries – buy organic | Refrigerate | Ellagic Acid in laboratory models inhibit certain tumor growth, second highest fruit with anthocyanins that inhibit the enzyme signaling pain and inflammation with arthritis, fiber, calcium, magnesium, phosphorus, potassium, Vit C, and Vit K |
| Cherries | | Ellagic Acid in laboratory models inhibit certain tumor growth, top fruit with anthocyanins that inhibit the enzyme signaling pain and inflammation with arthritis |
| Coconut | Countertop | Contains medium-chain saturated fatty acids (55% is lauric acid) antiviral, antibacterial |
| Grapes – buy organic | Refrigerate | Resveratrol in grape skin and seeds and associated with expression of three longevity genes, fiber, Vit C, Vit K |
| Mangoes | Countertop | Potassium, Vit A, beta-carotene, fiber, high in sugar but low glycemic load |
| Papaya<br>Black seeds in the interior of the fruit are edible and have a pepper-like, slightly bitter taste | Countertop | Papain a proteolytic enzyme that promotes protein digestion and anti-inflammatory, high in potassium, fiber, Vit C, Vit A, calcium, eye protecting lutein and zeaxanthin and beta-cryptoxanthine decreases risk of lung and colon cancer (carotenoids) |
| Cantaloupe | Countertop | High water and fiber content, Vit A, potassium |
| Honeydew | Countertop | High water and fiber content, potassium, few calories |
| Watermelon | Countertop | Lycopene may reduce cancer risk and beta-cryptoxanthine decreases risk of lung and colon cancer (carotenoids), Vit A, and 92% water, high sugar but low glycemic load |
| Kiwi | Countertop | 2X Vit C of oranges, Vit E, fiber, higher potassium than bananas, antioxidant |
| Avocado | Countertop | Oleic acid (MUFA) linked to a reduced risk of cancer and diabetes, lutein (eyes and skin), fiber, potassium, folate, Vit A |

| Tomatoes – buy organic (technically a berry, legally a vegetable) | Countertop | Lycopene which may provide protection against prostate, lung and stomach cancer (especially beneficial when consumed with fat-rich foods like avocado, nuts), zera-carotene, phytoene, phytofluene, phenolic acids, eye protecting lutein, Vit C (hothouse tomatoes have half the Vit C as vine-ripened), Vit A, Vit B-complex vitamins, calcium, potassium, phosphorus |
|---|---|---|
| Peaches/nectarines | Countertop | Fiber, small amounts of calcium, magnesium, phosphorus, Vit C, Vit K |
| Pears – buy organic | Countertop | Fiber (pectin), potassium |
| Cucumber – buy organic Cucurbitaceae plant family | Refrigerate | Vit K, molybdenum (cofactor of enzymes that process sulfites and breaking down toxins in the body), pantothenic acid, copper, potassium, manganese, Vit C, phosphorus, magnesium, biotin (B7), and Vit B1, silica (strengthens connective tissue and bones, supports healthy skin and hair) |

**DRIED FRUIT FOOD CHART** (all stored in the pantry in glass jars with lids or in resealable bags)

| DRIED FRUIT | NUTRITIONAL PROFILE |
|---|---|
| Dates | Go easy they have a high calorie and sugar content, but have a 1:1 ratio of calcium:magnesium, fiber, and potassium |
| Figs (1) | Fiber, 88-137mg calcium/5figs, potassium |
| Raisins (dried grapes so buy organic) | High in anti-oxidant phenols (higher than dates and figs), boron promoting bone and joint health, some calcium, magnesium, phosphorus, potassium, and fiber |
| Cranberries | Antioxidant, anticancer, antibacterial, high phenols |
| Cherries | Quercetin, Ellagic Acid |
| Apricots | Vit A, Vit C, fiber, copper, potassium |
| Mulberries | Protein, iron, Vit C, Vit K, fiber, potassium, phosphorus, calcium, antioxidants, resveratrol, eye protecting lutein and zeaxanthin |
| Goji Berries | Antioxidants, Vit A, Vit C, iron, and fiber |
| Sun-dried Tomatoes | Vit C, Vit K, iron, lycopene (carotenoid) may provide protection against prostate, lung and stomach cancer, potassium, copper, manganese |

Dried fruits retain most of the nutrient value of fresh fruit and have a long shelf life (will keep in the pantry for up to six months when properly stored). The major drawback is many brands contain added sugars – try to buy products where the ingredients are just fruit.

(1) **Fig puree:** healthier version of a sweetener or fat substitute. Combine 6-8 oz of fresh figs or dried figs (soaked) with ¼ to ⅓ cup of water in a blender or processor and store in the refrigerator.

# 16 — Recommended Foods

**GREENS FOOD CHART** (all require refrigeration and all should be organic)

| GREENS | NUTRITIONAL PROFILE |
|---|---|
| Romaine | Low in fiber but high in minerals, calcium, phosphorus, magnesium, potassium, Vitamins C, K, A (from beta-carotene) and B (folate) |
| Kale (a form of cabbage, brassica family of cruciferous vegetables) | 4g protein/2 cups, number one ORAC value (1770) among vegetables, two isothiocynates: indoles (have a protective effect against certain cancers) and sulforaphane (detoxification activity by supporting free radical removal through the liver), carotenoids (lutein and zeaxanthin), calcium, iron, beta-carotene that converts to Vit A (7X greater than broccoli), Vitamins A, C, K |
| Spinach Chenopod plant family | Vit K (one of the top sources), folate (Vit B), Vit C, Vit A, manganese, magnesium, iron, quercetin (anti-inflammatory compound), carotenoid – lutein (adding fat maximizes lutein absorption, so top spinach with olive oil), high in calcium but due to oxalic acid binding the calcium it has low bioavailability so not a good source |
| Cabbage brassica family of cruciferous vegetables | Indoles (isothiocynates) alters estrogen metabolism contributing to reduced cancer risk, anthocyanins (flavonoids) act as strong antioxidants and anti-inflammatory agents, calcium, magnesium, potassium, Vit C, K, A (from beta-carotene), fiber |
| Swiss Chard brassica family of cruciferous vegetables | Betalain (polyphenol), beta-carotene, lutein, zeaxanthin (carotenoids), quercetin and kaempferol (flavonols), potassium, magnesium, calcium, copper, manganese, iron, Vitamins K, A, B2, C, E |
| Collard Greens Cruciferous vegetables | 113mg calcium/½ cup, fiber, calcium, folate, maganese, magnesium, phosphorus, potassium, Vit C, K, A in the form of beta-carotene, lutein, zeaxanthin (carotenoids) |
| Mustard Greens brassica family | Vit K, A, C, folate, manganese, fiber, calcium, oxalate (have been shown to interfere with calcium absorption) |
| Radicchio chicory | Selenium, iron, copper, phosphorus, manganese, potassium, phosphorus, calcium, zinc, inulin (regulates blood sugar levels), fiber, polyphenols, lutein and zeaxanthin (carotenoids), Vitamins B, folate, A, C, K, E.  Lactucopicrin gives radicchio its bitter taste, antimalarial, and analgesic effects |
| Arugula Cruciferous vegetables | Low calorie: 5 calories/1 cup, folate, Vit A, lutein, zeaxanthin (carotenoids), calcium (equals spinach levels without oxalates that inhibit absorption), Vit K, contain glucosinolates that react to form isothiocyanates with anticancer properties |

**VEGETABLE FOOD CHART** (store in refrigerator, unless otherwise indicated)

| VEGETABLES | NUTRITIONAL PROFILE |
|---|---|
| Broccoli (2)<br>brassica family of cruciferous vegetables | Indole-3-carbinol (reduces the risk of breast and cervical cancer) and sulforaphane (both isothiocynates) have anti-carcinogenic properties, potassium, calcium, Vitamins C and A (from beta-carotene), folate, magnesium, phosphorus |
| Cauliflower<br>brassica family | Indoles and sulforaphane (both isothiocynates) have anti-carcinogenic properties, fiber, Vit C, potassium, folate |
| Sweet Peppers (1) – buy organic<br>Red (the sweetest of the bell peppers that starts out green and ripens into a red color)<br>Yellow, Orange, Green | Vitamins C, K, A (beta-carotene), potassium, lycopene (carotenoid) may provide protection against prostate, lung and stomach cancer |
| Brussel Sprouts<br>brassica family of cruciferous vegetables | Two isothiocyanates: sulforaphane (anti-carcinogenic) and inigrin (suppresses precancerous cells) and breaks down to an isothiocyanate responsible for the smell of brussel sprouts, folate, potassium, Vit K |
| Zucchini (1)<br>Cucurbitaceae plant family<br>Summer squash (lower in calories and sugar than other squash) | Low glycemic index, potassium, manganese, Vitamins C, A (alpha and beta-carotene), B (folate, B6, riboflavin), fiber (pectin), lutein and zeaxanthin (carotenoids), high volume food (high water content, filling and low calorie) |
| Yellow Squash (yellow zucchini) (1)<br>Summer squash (lower in calories and sugar than other squash) | Low glycemic index, potassium, Vitamins C, A (beta-carotene), B (folate), fiber (pectin), manganese, high volume food (high water content, filling and low calorie) |
| Acorn squash (pepper squash) (1)<br>Winter squash (higher in carbohydrate than other squash) | 9g fiber/1 cup, Vit C, A (beta-carotene), fiber, potassium, iron, lutein and zeaxanthin (only in raw squash), high volume food (high water content, filling and low calorie) |
| Butternut Squash<br>Winter squash (higher in carbohydrate than other squash) | Vit A powerehouse (22,868 IU's/1 cup) – contains both alpha and beta-carotene Vit. A precursors, beta-cryptoxanthin (carotenoid) that my lower the risk of lung cancer, high volume food (high water content, filling and low calorie) |
| Spaghetti squash<br>Winter squash (higher in carbohydrate than other squash) | Lowest calorie winter squash (42 calories/1 cup), lower in fiber, potassium, Vit A, high volume food (high water content, filling and low calorie) |
| Pumpkin (1) fresh/canned<br>Winter squash | 564mg potassium (30% more than a banana), 12,000 IU's of Vit. A, Carotenoids: alpha and beta-carotene - precursors of Vit A and beta-cryptoxanthin (strong antioxidant and associated with a reduced risk of lung cancer and rheumatoid arthritis) and lutein and zeaxanthin, 2.5g fiber/1 cup, trace amounts of calcium, iron, magnesium, phosphorus |
| Edamame - buy organic<br>(see soybeans in Legumes/Soy/ Fermented Soy/Grains Food Chart) | (see soybeans in Legumes/Soy/Fermented Soy/Grains Food Chart) |
| Eggplant (1)<br>Nightshade Family | Nasunin (anthocyanin) – strong antioxidant, low calorie, high fiber, potassium calcium, magnesium, phosphorus, niacin, folate, phytosterols |
| Asparagus | High in potassium and folate, Vit K, rutin (protects blood vessels), quercetin (flavonol), fiber(inulin – supports G.I. health), saponins (support inhibition of cancer cells), glutathione (antioxidant), low in calories. The characteristic, harmless odor it causes in your urine is due to the amino acid asparagine |
| Carrots | 30,000 IU's of Vit A (6,000 IU's alpha and 15,000 IU's beta-carotene), eye protecting carotenoids lutein and zeaxanthin, calcium, potassium, fiber, regarding sugar content - glycemic load is actually low |

| | |
|---|---|
| Red beets - buy organic<br>Chenopod plant family | Betacyanin – gives beets their red color and makes your urine red after beet consumption, betaine and folate work synergistically to promote cardiovascular health by reducing the amino acid homocysteine that can damage blood vessels, 528g of potassium, magnesium. Beet leaves have even higher nutritional value in calcium, iron, Vitamins A and C |
| Golden beets - buy organic<br>Chenopod plant family | Sweeter than red beets with less earthy flavor, beta-carotene (Vit A), lycopene, folate, Vit C, potassium, calcium, flavonoids, eye protecting carotenoid zeaxanthin, fiber |
| Celery – buy organic | Quercetin (flavonol), caffeic acid and ferulic acid (phenolic acids), 3-n-butylphthalide (has lipid-lowering properties), Vitamins K, C, B6, potassium, folate, polyacetylenes (reduce toxicity, fight against cancer formation), nutrient dense but low in calories, promotes diuresis |
| Snow Peas (1) | 5g fiber/1 cup, 2098 IUs of Vit A (126 IU's of beta carotene), Vit K, eye protecting carotenoids lutein and zeaxanthin, calcium, potassium, Vit C, folate |
| Yams/Sweet potato (3)<br>(store on countertop)<br>Morning Glory family | Fiber (50% soluble), beta-carotene Vit. A precursor, quercetin (flavonol), chlorogenic acid (polyphenol) has antioxidant and anticarcinogenic properties, moderate glycemic load, potassium, calcium |
| Onion – allium family includes scallions, chives, leeks<br>(store on countertop) | Diallyl sulfide (increases production of cancer-fighting enzyme, glutathione-S-transferase), sulfur compounds that help decrease the tendency for clots to form (promote cardiovascular health), quercetin (flavonol). Leeks: eye protecting carotenoids lutein and zeaxanthin |
| Garlic<br>(store on countertop) | Diallyl sulfide (increases production of cancer-fighting enzyme, glutathione-S-transferase), allicin (antithrombotic: prevents platelets from sticking together supporting prevention of heart attacks and stroke), antihypertensive, antioxidant, antimicrobial, antiviral, antiparasitic |

(1) Technically a fruit, but most people classify as vegetables so placed in this chart for locating easily

(2) Low oxalate

(3) Yams/sweet potatoes are not actually related to the potato. The orange flesh colored variety is commonly referred to as yams (but are still not a true yam, not commonly found in the U.S.) and is moist and sweeter than the yellow flesh

**LEGUMES/SOY/FERMENTED SOY/GRAINS FOOD CHART** (highest protein sources). Legumes are the world's second most important source of calories and protein, after grains. Included in this category: beans, lentils, peas

| LEGUMES/SOY/GRAINS | KITCHEN STORAGE | AMOUNT OF WATER/ONE CUP OF LEGUME OR GRAIN | NUTRITIONAL PROFILE |
|---|---|---|---|
| Beans, canned (1) Garbanzo, Black, Pinto, White beans: Cannellini (large, mild flavor, creamy) Great Northern (smaller, grainy, nutty flavor) Navy or Boston (small, cook quickly, good for soups) | Pantry (once can is opened, store unused beans in a glass container in the refrigerator) | Fully cooked | 14-15.8g protein/1 cup, high in fiber, anticancer effects from fiber and diosgenin, saponins, protease inhibitors, ultimate low glycemic food, lowers cholesterol, contains potassium, copper, phosphorus, manganese, magnesium, iron, thiamine (Vit B1), folate (Vit B9), riboflavin (Vit B2), Vit B6. Can be high in sodium - often added in the canning process, so rinse well directly out of the can to reduce sodium as much as 41% |
| Beans, dried (2) | Pantry (once cooked, store unused portion in a glass container in the refrigerator) | 4 cups water/1 cup beans, cook for 1.5-2.5 hours, depending on type of bean | See Beans, canned |
| Lentils (3) (Dahl is a dish from India of lentils cooked to a puree with curry.) | Pantry (once cooked, store unused portion in a glass container in the refrigerator) | 3 cups water/1 cup lentils, cook for 25 minutes | 18g protein/1 cup, 6.6mg iron/1 cup, high fiber, low glycemic load, folate, iron, manganese, don't contain sulfur like beans so don't produce gas |
| Peas | Pantry or Freezer | Boil 2-3 minutes in minimum water or steam 1-2 minutes | 5g protein/½ cup, very high in Vitamins A and K, and fiber |
| Soy Beans, cooked (aka, edamame) Consume as a high protein snack or in a dip | Refrigerate/Freeze | 4 cups water/1 cup soy beans, cook for 3+ hours | 28.6g protein/1 cup (highest protein), 175mg calcium/1 cup, 8.8mg iron/1 cup, fiber, magnesium, folate, potassium |
| Mung Bean/Sprouts (green legume in the pea and lentil plant family) | Refrigerate | 3 cups water/1 cup mung beans, boil 5 minutes, cover and let stand 4-5 minutes. Rinse sprouts in a colander without disturbing the sprout portion and add to salads for crunch. | 14g protein/1 cup, fiber, manganese, potassium, magnesium, folate, copper, zinc, and various B Vitamins, antioxidants, and phytonutrients Sprouting releases enzymes making the beans more digestible, 3g protein/cup |
| Tofu | Refrigerate | | 20g protein/½ cup, 861mg calcium/½ cup |
| Tempeh (fermented soy) Traditional Indonesian food made from controlled fermentation of cooked whole soybeans | Refrigerate | | 15.8g protein/½ cup, soy protein and isoflavones may reduce the risk of heart disease and some cancers, the fermentation process produces natural antibiotic agents believed to increase resistance to infection. |
| Miso (fermented soy) A soybean paste (cooked soybeans with salt, a grain, and a fermenting agent called koji) used In Japanese cooking | Refrigerate | | 8g protein/¼ cup, selenium, potassium, phosphorus, fiber, high amount of sodium |

| Food | Storage | Cooking | Nutrition |
|---|---|---|---|
| Brown rice (white rice has the bran layer removed and is less nutritious, while brown rice only has the outer hull removed retaining nutrients) | Pantry (once cooked, store unused portion in a glass container in the refrigerator) | 2 cups water/1 cup rice, cook for 45 minutes | 4.5g protein/1 cup medium grain (long grain 5g protein), fiber, niacin, Vit B6, magnesium, manganese, phosphorus, selenium, high glycemic impact |
| Oatmeal (different types see step Three, Breakfast Choices, Grains) | Pantry (once cooked, store unused portion in a glass container in the refrigerator) | Rolled: 3 cups water/1 cup oats, cook for 10 minutes Steel cut: 3 cups water/1 cup oats, cook for 30-40 minutes | 6.75g protein/½ cup whole oats (lower protein in quick and instant varieties), fiber, manganese, magnesium, phosphorus, zinc, selenium, iron, folate, copper |
| Buckwheat groats (4) (actually classified as a seed, not a grain, the hulled seeds of the buckwheat plant) | Pantry (once cooked, store unused portion in a glass container in the refrigerator) | 3 cups water/1 cup groats, cook for 1 hour | 6g protein/¼ cup, higher in protein than any rice or millet and contains two essential amino acids lysine and arginine, gluten-free, high in flavonoids especially rutin important for cardiovascular health, high in antioxidants and fiber, low glycemic index, contains B vitamins/folate, magnesium, phosphorus, manganese, zinc, iron |
| Millet (grain-like seed) Gluten-free, described as a grain, but actually a seed | Pantry (once cooked, store unused portion in a glass container in the refrigerator) | 3 cups water/1 cup millet, cook for 20 minutes | 4.2g protein/½ cup, gluten- free, Vit B, calcium, fiber, magnesium, phosphorus, manganese, antioxidants |
| Wheat berries (chewy texture, whole grain containing germ, endosperm, bran) | Pantry (once cooked, store unused portion in a glass container in the refrigerator) | 3 cups water/1 cup wheatberries, cook for 1 hour | 6.5g protein/½ cup, fiber, Vit B1, Vit B3, magnesium, phosphorus, copper, manganese, selenium |
| Quinoa Chenopod plant family (Commonly referred to as a grain, but actually a seed) | Pantry (once cooked, store unused portion in a glass container in the refrigerator) | 2 cups water/1 cup quinoa, cook for 20 minutes | 8g protein/cup including all nine essential amino acids (lysine not in many other grains), higher in iron than any other grain, fiber, calcium, phosphorus, magnesium, potassium, copper, manganese, zinc |

(1) Buy canned beans from manufacturers that don't use cans lined with BPA

(2) Rinse dried beans repeatedly, then soak overnight prior to cooking or quick-soak by boiling 2 cups of beans in 10 cups of water for 2-3 minutes, remove from heat, cover and let stand for at least 1 hour. Follow cooking directions

(3) Lentils don't require pre-soaking like beans. Red lentils cook the quickest and the soft texture is best for purees, brown and green lentils maintain their shape after cooking so better for salads when you want texture.

(4) Buckwheat groat preparation (use two large bowls and a colander): soak groats in a large bowl of water (1:2 ratio) for a total of 4-6 hours, repeatedly drain, rinse (placing small batches of groats in a colander and stream water over them), replace in a second large bowl and refill soak water, repeat two to three times. Cover with saran wrap and refrigerate during soak period. Continue until minimal amount of sticky white material remains and do a final thorough rinse. Now groats are ready for cooking or dehydrating (advanced plant-based use).

**SEEDS FOOD CHART** (purchase all as organic) Include a daily consumption of ½ to ⅔ cup combination of nuts and seeds (dependent on your desire to lose or maintain weight since they are high in calories). Seeds are more nutritious than nuts when comparing protein and mineral content. Their fat content also enhances mineral absorption and makes for a creamy nut/seed butter when they release their oils while in a food processor.

| SEEDS | KITCHEN STORAGE | NUTRITIONAL PROFILE |
|---|---|---|
| Pumpkin | Pantry in glass jars w/ lids or resealable bag | 8.5g protein/¼ cup, 5.2mg iron/¼ cup, phytosterols (promote lowering cholesterol), magnesium, potassium, phosphorus, manganese, fiber, selenium |
| Sunflower | Pantry in glass jars w/ lids or resealable bag | 8.0g protein/¼ cup, phytosterols (helps lower cholesterol), selenium and Vit E (work synergistically to fight cancer), fiber, potassium, magnesium, phosphorus, iron, manganese, copper, zinc. Source of betaine (helps lower an amino acid risk factor for heart disease) |
| Hemp (These seeds come from the hemp plant, contain a trace amount of THC (active ingredient in marijuana) and they will NOT get you high, are safe and healthy to eat) | Pantry in glass jars w/ lids or resealable bag | 9.2g protein/1 oz (contains all essential amino acids), perfect balance omega-3:omega-6 fatty acids at a ratio of 3:1 to promote cardiovascular health (includes gamma-linolenic acid, GLA which helps balance hormones), fiber, Vit E, phosphorus, potassium, magnesium, calcium, iron, zinc |
| Chia | Refrigerate | 4.4g protein/1 oz, antioxidants, fatty acids (linoleic acid and alpha-linolenic acid - ALA) more omega-3's than salmon, calcium, potassium, magnesium, manganese, phosphorus, zinc, copper, selenium |
| Flaxseed (linseeds), whole and meal Flaxseeds best consumed ground, whole seeds pass through the G.I. tract undigested | Refrigerate | 6g protein/1 oz, richest source of plant-based omega-3 fatty acids (alpha-linolenic acid, ALA), lignans (antioxidants that support the immune system and balance hormones), fiber (mucilage gel-forming fiber increases G.I. nutrient absorption), magnesium, Vit B1, manganese, phosphorus, selenium |
| Sesame | Pantry in glass jars w/ lids or resealable bag | Sesame lignans: sesamin and sesaminol (antioxidants that support the immune system, balance hormones, enhance Vit E absorption, improve lipid profiles, and help to maintain a healthy blood pressure), cholesterol phytosterols, calcium (limited availability due to binding to oxalic acid), fiber, protein (more than any other seed or nut), copper, iron, magnesium, phosphorus, potassium, manganese |
| Tahini-sesame seed butter* Made from hulled (removing the outer skin) sesame seeds. Tahini also an ingredient in hummus (middle Eastern dip, see Dressings/Dips in Step Three) | Refrigerate after opening jar | 8.1g protein/3 tbsp 50-191mg calcium/3 tbsp See nutritional benefits for sesame seeds **\* Tahini (sesame seed butter) – listed in discussion of nut/seed butters under the Nut section below** |
| Wheatgerm (Germ is the smallest portion of the four components of whole grain, rich in vitamins, minerals, and fiber). Nutty flavor, crunchy texture. Gluten product | Refrigerate after open and use within a few months (due to high in oil can go rancid if not properly stored) | 6g protein/¼cup, one of the highest phytosterol counts (helps lower cholesterol), fiber, zinc, calcium, iron, magnesium, phosphorus, potassium, Vit E/selenium, folate, Vit B (niacin, thiamine, B6), manganese |
| Quinoa | Pantry in glass jars w/ lids or resealable bag | See Grains Food Chart |

**NUTS FOOD CHART** (all stored in the pantry in glass jars with lids or resealable bags and purchase all as organic). Nuts contain the amino acid arginine which acts to protect the inner lining of the arterial walls so they are more pliable decreasing the opportunity for plaque formation. Most nuts contain monounsaturated fatty acids (MUFA) and walnuts contain polyunsaturated fat (PUFA), the majority in the form of omega-3 fatty acids. Their fat content also enhances mineral absorption and makes for a creamy nut/seed butter when they release their oils while combining in a food processor.

| NUTS | NUTRITIONAL PROFILE |
| --- | --- |
| Walnuts | Contain the highest omega-3 of any other nut, protein, fiber, calcium, magnesium, phosphorus, potassium. manganese |
| Pistachios | MUFA, phytosterols (helps lower cholesterol), high potassium:sodium ratio helping to normalize blood pressure, protein, Vit E, thiamin, Vit B6, magnesium, copper, iron, phosphorus, kernel extract shows antiviral activity |
| Almonds | MUFA, 7.4g protein/ ¼ cup – complete protein, fiber, calcium, phosphorus, Vit E, magnesium |
| Cashews | MUFA, slightly lower in calories and highest carbohydrate content of any nut, protein, Vit E, Vit K, Vit B6, copper, calcium, selenium, potassium, phosphorus, zinc, magnesium, iron and fiber |
| Brazil nuts | MUFA, highest selenium content of any food, protein, calcium, fiber, |
| Pecans - Refrigerate or freeze (for up to one year) due to high oil content, can go rancid when not refrigerated | MUFA, potassium, Vit E, phytosterols (helps lower cholesterol), fiber |
| Macadamia nuts | Highest MUFA of any other nut and very high in calories, calcium, phosphorus, magnesium, potassium fiber, small amount of selenium, phytosterols (helps lower cholesterol and promotes prostate health) |

**Nut butters:** an excellent source of fiber and healthy unsaturated plant-based fats. You will find a recipe for this in the book so you won't have to worry about buying a product that may have added sugar or high fructose corn syrup. I don't recommend peanut butter because peanuts are susceptible to contamination. They are technically legumes and not nuts, so they have a soft permeable pod rather than a hard, protective shell, like nuts. They also grow underground which makes them more susceptible to mold growth. One of the molds associated with peanuts produces aflatoxin which is a known carcinogen associated with liver cancer.

> **Almond butter, nut/seed butters (see Dena's Power Nut/Seed Butter in the Breakfast recipe section), plus tahini (sesame seed butter)**

**Nut milks (almond, hemp, combination nut milks):** search for brands that only contain the featured nut and filtered water. Some products contain food additives such as carrageenan, gums, and food starches to thicken the product and make it appear more like dairy milk.

**SPICES/HERBS FOOD CHART.** Spices and herbs are used to add flavor to foods and have positive biological effects on our health either independently or synergistically with phytochemicals from plants.

| SPICE/HERB | NUTRITIONAL PROFILE |
|---|---|
| Basil | Antimicrobial, anti-inflammatory, antioxidants (flavonoids – vicenin, orientin, eugenol, anthocyanins), Vit K, zinc, calcium, magnesium, potassium, fiber |
| Black Pepper | Stimulates taste buds which incites production of stomach acid and improves digestion, anti-nausea properties |
| Cilantro/ Coriander | Once cilantro flowers it produces coriander seeds, Vitmins A, C, E, K, folate, potassium, magnesium, calcium, iron, fiber, binds toxic metals, antioxidant |
| Dill | Vitamins A, C, niacin, riboflavin, B6, folate, manganese, iron, calcium, phosphorus, copper, magnesium, flavonoids (kaempferol, vicenin ), antibacterial, antifungal, promotes neutralization of carcinogens |
| Cardamom | Carminative (digestive aid) – an agent that moves gas from the stomach to intestines, stimulates bile flow, limonene (boosts the synthesis of an enzyme with antioxidant properties) |
| Cinnamon | Anthocyanins, chalcone polymers (increase glucose metabolism), eugenol and geraniol (antibacterial properties), carminative (digestive aid), catechins (relieve nausea) |
| Clove | Eugenol (antibacterial properties), antiseptic, anesthetic (clove oil historically used to relieve tooth aches), manganese, calcium, potassium, phytosterols, fiber |
| Cumin | Relieves allergic symptoms, reduces heartburn, relieves indigestion, antimicrobial (essential oil portion of the seed), iron, magnesium, potassium, calcium |
| Curry | Made up of numerous ingredients (turmeric, coriander, cardamom, cumin, basil, pepper and may have fennel seeds, ginger, garlic, cinnamon, mustard seeds), curcumin from turmeric, anti-cancer activity, anti-inflammatory, antibacterial, anticoagulant properties |
| Mustard Seeds | Allyl isothiocyanates (play a role in suppressing tumor growth), stimulate circulation, neutralize toxins. Mustard Seeds are a member of the brassica family (cruciferous vegetables). |
| Garlic | Allicin (anti-platelet activity promoting cardiovascular health and antibacterial properties), lipid-lowering, antihypertensive, antioxidant properties |
| Ginger | Gingerol (gives ginger its characteristic flavor and antiemetic properties preventing nausea and vomiting), zingerone and shogaol (antioxidant and anti-inflammatory properties), improves circulation, antimicrobial, antiviral |
| Himalayan Sea Salt | Sodium chloride, magnesium, potassium, calcium, iron, zinc, contain 84 minerals that are good for your health |
| Oregano | Calcium, magnesium, zinc, iron, potassium, copper, boron, manganese, Vitamins C, A and niacin, highest antioxidant activity of any herb (42X more than apples, 12X more than oranges, and 4X more than blueberries). Oregano oil contains thymol and carvacrol (antifungal, antibacterial, antiparastic), rosmarinic acid (anticarcinogenic). The oil is used as a digestive aid and due to anti-inflammatory properties to support joint function |
| Paprika | Made from air-dried bell peppers and/or chili and cayenne peppers, variety of carotenoids, Vitamins A, B6, E |
| Parsley | Contains chlorophyll (detoxifying and deodorizing properties), myristicin (from the oils in parsley, may inhibit tumors), lutein and zeaxanthin (eye-protecting carotenoids), beta-carotene, Vitamins K and A |
| Rosemary | Rosmarinic acid (anticarcinogenic), caffeic acid (anti-inflammatory), diterpenes, monoterpenes, Vit E, prevent breakdown of neurotransmitters in the brain to support brain function and memory |
| Sumac* | Lemony-flavored spice from the dried red berries of the sumac plant, Vit C, protein, fiber, potassium, calcium, magnesium, phosphorus, tannins (astringent properties), antioxidant, antimicrobial, antifungal, tangy flavor comes from the presence of a variety of acids (malic, gallic, citric, fumaric, and ascorbic) |
| Thyme | Thymol (found in the herb's oil has antiseptic, antioxidant, and anti-inflammatory properties), digestive aid |
| Turmeric | Curcumin (anti-inflammatory, antitumor, and antioxidant properties) |
| Vanilla* | Vanillin (chief chemical component), small amounts of B-complex vitamins, small traces of calcium, magnesium, potassium, manganese, iron, and zinc . **See section below, "More on Nutritional Superstars and Other Supplements"** |

All spices/herbs you purchase should be organic. Greater than 50% of spices are imported and fall under the governmental sterilization requirement to be sold in the U.S. The only sterilization technique approved for certified organic items is steaming, which destroys bacteria while retaining flavor and nutrients of the spices. The most common method of sterilization of conventionally grown spices is fumigation, which can utilize a variety of chemicals that result in residue leftover on spices. There are no labeling requirements to inform the consumer if this process was conducted. If spices are irradiated (the third form of sterilization), it can reduce the flavor and nutrients of the spices. Conclusion: either buy organic to ensure the spices are steam sterilized or grow your own.

### Some Information About Oils—How do oils effect cardiovascular function?

The vessels in our bodies are lined with endothelial cells. One of the functions of these cells is to make blood vessels dilate to increase blood flow and prevent platelets from sticking to cell walls and constricting blood flow. Impaired endothelial function is considered a hallmark of vascular disease. Ultimately, all oils, including olive oil have been shown to cause a significant decrease in endothelial function (arteries stiffen and the ability to dilate is impaired) after consumption. The Mediterranean diet (with high olive oil intake) has been promoted as healthy because it is rich in vegetables which when consumed with a meal high in oil, the vegetables partially compensate for the damaging blood vessel effects by the oil in that they support restoration of arterial function. With that scientific knowledge base, the goal should be to consume the smallest amount of oil in your diet. It is important to know the basics about oils.

Oils are extracted from nuts, seeds, olives, grains, and legumes by chemicals or mechanically. Refined (processed) oils are treated with chemicals such as an acid or purified with an alkali and it can also be neutralized, filtered, or deodorized with chemicals like hexane. The refining process causes oxidation of the oils resulting in trans fats. For example, unrefined oils like extra virgin olive oil are processed by machine only which helps to maintain the antioxidants. Cold-pressing preserves flavor of heat-sensitive oils and retains polyphenols, plant sterols, and Vitamin E. When choosing an oil, buy organic, unrefined, and cold-pressed.

Smoke point is the temperature at which an oil begins to produce a continuous bluish smoke and is an indicator of which oils are better for high heat cooking/frying. When you cook with an oil that's been heated past its smoke point it destroys nutrients and phytochemicals in the oil and creates harmful free radicals. The more refined (processed) an oil, generally the higher the smoke point. Unrefined oils (flaxseed and walnut oils) have a low smoke point and should not be heated.

The top six oils you should completely avoid include: canola, vegetable oil, soybean, safflower, and corn. Also, avoid all hydrogenated oils (Crisco and margarine) which results in healthy fats being converted to trans fats. The more solid the fat the more hydrogenated it is.

**OIL FOOD CHART**

| OIL | Smoke Point °C | Omega-6 : Omega-3 ratio | NUTRITIONAL PROFILE |
|---|---|---|---|
| Avocado Oil | 520° | 12:1 | Suitable for cooking at high heat, 72-76% monounsaturated fat (helps to maintain a healthy blood pressure), one of the few oils not derived from seeds, oleic acid (omega-9 that reduces the risk of heart disease by raising HDL good cholesterol), Vitamin E |
| Coconut Oil | 350° | | Not suitable for cooking at high heat, 86% of its fatty acids are saturated predominately *lauric acid* which has antimicrobial, antibacterial, and antiviral properties. Contains 66% healthy medium-chain triglycerides (raises LDL blood cholesterol but compensates by ability to raise HDL or good cholesterol) |
| Flaxseed Oil | 225° | 1:4 | Not suitable for cooking/frying, high in alpha-linolenic acid (an essential omega-3 fatty acid), a good balance of other fatty acids (omega-6 and omega-9), lignans - antioxidants that support the immune system and balance hormones |
| Grapeseed Oil | 420° | 676:1 | Good for sautéing over medium-high heat, 4mg/tbsp, predominately omega-6 fatty acids (not all promote inflammation – grapeseed oil lowers inflammation and insulin resistance), 70% polyunsaturated fat, linoleic acid (helps lower cholesterol and inflammation and reduces cardiovascular disease), Vit E (good for hair and skin) |
| Hemp Oil | 330° | 3:1 | Not suitable for cooking at high heat, best omega-6:omega-3 ratio of any oil, gamma-linolenic acid (the only seed with this important omega-6 fatty acid), promote cardiovascular health, anti-inflammatory |
| Olive Oil Extra Virgin (result of the first pressing) | 405° | 13:1 | Good for sautéing over medium-high heat, 74% monounsaturated fat (71.3% Omega-9), Vit E, polyphenols |
| Sesame Oil | 350° | 138:1 | Good for light sautéing, despite being high in omega-6 fatty acids it has many potential health benefits, 40% monounsaturated fats, sesamol, sesamin, sesamolin (antioxidants, inhibit production of inflammatory compounds), associated with lowering blood pressure |
| Walnut Oil | 320° | 5:1 | Not suitable for cooking/frying, 1.4g/1 tbsp alpha -linolenic acid (ALA) an omega-3-fatty acid providing cardio-protective benefits, ellagic acid (phenolic acid/polyphenol - antioxidant, anti-inflammatory, and anticarcinogenic activities antioxidants) |

Compare statistics on highly processed oils that are not recommended: Canola Oil (3:1, undergoes high temperature mechanical pressing and solvent extraction turning the valuable omega-3's into trans fats, when put in products, it is hydrogenated, increasing shelf life but also the trans fat content, 80% of Canola in U.S. is GMO), Safflower Oil (133:1 and 74% Omega-9), Corn Oil (83:1), Sunflower Oil (40:1), Palm Kernel Oil (82% saturated and no omega-3), Peanut Oil (32:1)

## CONDIMENTS FOOD CHART

| CONDIMENT | NUTRITIONAL PROFILE |
| --- | --- |
| Apple Cider Vinegar (2) | Acetic acid, potassium, magnesium, phosphorus, fluorine, probiotics, and enzymes, and pectin. It has been reported to help with acid reflux, lower blood pressure, improve diabetes and support weight loss |
| Balsamic Vinegar (2) | Made from pressed or fermented grapes, flavonoids from grapes, calcium, magnesium, zinc, phosphorus, potassium, sodium, polyphenols (stabilize cholesterol levels), low glycemic index |
| Bragg's Liquid Aminos (1) | Soy sauce alternative rich in amino acids (protein source), contains soy, made from non-GMO soybeans, gluten-free, high levels of sodium but due to concentrated flavor you can use less than traditional soy sauce |
| Coconut Aminos (1) | Soy sauce alternative, comes from the sap of coconut trees, soy-free, gluten-free, lower sodium, additional amino acids, a bit sweeter flavor as compared to traditional soy sauce |
| Honey, raw, unfiltered | One of the best sweeteners to use keeping in mind that it is sugar but contains nutrients including: Vit B6, Vit C, riboflavin, fluoride, flavonoids, does not contain fat |
| Lemon Juice | Calcium, potassium, and Vit C |
| Lime Juice | Potassium, antioxidant (flavonoids) and anti-bacterial properties |
| Maple Syrup | As compared to honey: less overall sugar and less fructose (35%), more minerals (iron, calcium, magnesium, zinc, manganese, potassium), and lower calorie count. Contains B Vitamins, fat, and antioxidant properties |
| Miso | Fermented paste used in Japanese cuisine, made from legumes and sometimes grains and contains friendly bacteria. Miso is available in different colors: dark has a deep salty flavor, light-colored miso is a combination of sweet and salty |
| Molasses, BlackStrap (buy unsulfured) | Sweetener that is low in sugar and high in nutrients, robust bitter-tart flavor, dark on color, contains iron, B vitamins, potassium, calcium (176mg calcium/1 tbsp), magnesium, manganese, copper, and small amounts of selenium |
| Mustard | Made from the seeds of the mustard plant, calcium, magnesium, phosphorus, potassium, folate, Vit A, and phenolic components found in the seeds, leaves and oils of mustard plants, oxalate (known to interfere with calcium absorption) |
| Tamari (1) | Soy sauce alternative, Japanese sauce, contains soy, wheat-free (gluten-free), fermented, lower in sodium |

(1) Soy sauce contains soy which may be an allergen for some people, gluten, and high levels of sodium - soy sauce alternatives might be a better option

(2) Vinegar can be made from any fruit or sugar material that can be fermented to less than 18% ethyl alcohol. To be labeled as a vinegar, the product must contain at least 4% acidity. Pasteurized vinegar destroys heat-sensitive vitamins and enzymes and distilled vinegar is not much better. Buy vinegars that are labeled: unpasteurized, traditionally fermented or brewed, and unfiltered.

**ALGAE AND SEAWEED CHART:** Algae and seaweed are sea vegetables. Seaweed is not a viable source of Vitamin B1, and all sea weeds listed are of Japanese origin, except dulse which is of Gaelic origin.

| PRODUCT | ALGAE OR SEAWEED | NUTRITIONAL PROFILE |
|---|---|---|
| Chlorella (micro-algae, sold as powder supplement) | Green Algae | Chlorophyll, 50% complete protein, heavy metal detoxification properties, rich in nucleic acids, beta-carotene, stimulates good aerobic bacterial growth beneficial to bowel health |
| Spirulina (micro-algae, sold as powder supplement) | Blue-green Algae (cyanobacteria) | Chlorophyll, 70% complete protein, cell wall is easily broken down so nutrients are readily bioavailable, Vit B12 (one of few plant sources), gamma linolenic acid (GLA) an omega-6 fatty acid (other foods provide linoleic acid that is later converted to GLA in the body), phycocyanin (phytochemical) gives spirulina its blue hue and antioxidant properties |
| Dulse (sea lettuce flakes) | Seaweed | Fluorine, selenium, Vitamins A, C, E, B6, B12, calcium, iodine, magnesium, protein, fiber |
| Kombu* (Kelp Family) | Seaweed | Sodium alginate (protective against radiation), fucoidan a polysaccharide with anticancer activities, fluorine, selenium, iodine, iron (four times the iron of beef), potassium, calcium, Vitamins A and C, iodine (100-500 times more than shellfish) **\*When added to a pot of beans, Kombu speeds up the cooking process and increases the digestibility of beans (decreases G.I. gas production).** |
| Wakame (Kelp Family) | Seaweed | Sodium alginate (protective against radiation), fucoidan a polysaccharide with anticancer activities, fluorine, selenium, iodine, iron (four times the iron of beef), protein, calcium (more than ten times the calcium from milk), iron (four times the iron of beef) |
| Hijiki | Seaweed | Sodium alginate (protective against radiation), fluorine, selenium, the most calcium of any sea vegetable, iron (eight times the iron of beef), Vit A. Higher risk sea vegetable of arsenic exposure due to heavy metals in waters where they grow – safe if purchase certified organic hijiki |
| Arame (Kelp Family) | Seaweed | Sodium alginate (protective against radiation), fluorine, selenium, iodine (100-500 times more iodine than from shellfish), iron (four times the iron of beef), Vit A, calcium (ten times the calcium from milk) |
| Nori (used in sushi) | Seaweed | Fluorine, selenium, protein, calcium, iron, potassium, Vit A (more than contained in carrots) |

## MISCELLANEOUS PRODUCTS

| MISCELLANEOUS PRODUCTS | NUTRITIONAL PROFILE |
|---|---|
| Nutritional yeast (flakes) | 9g protein/¼ cup, a complete protein source, B vitamins (folates, thiamine, riboflavin, niacin), one of the few vegan food sources of B12, selenium, zinc, fiber, gluten-free |
| Coconut Flakes | 10g fat/¼ cup (9g medium-chain saturated fat which raises good and bad cholesterol), iron (eat coconut flakes with a food rich in Vit C to enhance absorption), phosphorus, zinc, fiber |
| Cacao Powder Cacao Nibs (unsweetened) Dark Chocolate (70-85% cacao) | Antioxidant properties (four times that of dark chocolate and more than twenty times that of blueberries), theobromine, protein, calcium, carotene, thiamine, riboflavin, magnesium, sulfur, iron, copper, manganese, flavonoids (improves cholesterol levels and lowers blood pressure), essential fatty acids, 1g sugar/½ cup raw cacao, phenolic phytochemicals (theaflavin, resveratrol), increases serotonin levels (boosts your mood) |

**BAKING SUPPLIES/PRODUCTS**

| BAKING PRODUCT | NUTRITIONAL PROFILE |
|---|---|
| Coconut Sugar (Coconut palm sugar) | Low glycemic sweetener (glycemic index 35), 3-9% fructose and glucose (cane sugar is 50% fructose), minimal amounts iron, zinc, calcium |
| Brown Rice Flour | High in amino acids, gluten-free, choline, makes baked products fluffier than when using wheat flour, fiber, lower in folate and fewer phytonutrients than wheat flour |
| Coconut Flour | Fiber, protein, healthy medium-chain fatty acids, gluten-free, low in sugar, may have to add extra liquid to recipes when substituting with coconut flour |
| Oat Four | Fiber, thiamin, iron, calcium, potassium |
| Spelt Flour | Wheat flour alternative (better tolerated by those sensitive to wheat than wheat flour), copper, iron, zinc, magnesium, phosphorus, thiamine, niacin, manganese, fiber |
| Sucanat | Sweetener that retains natural molasses color and flavor, minimal amounts potassium, iron, calcium, Vit B6 |

## Plant-based Protein Powders

A balanced, quality plant-based diet will provide you with the amount of protein your body needs to function. However, there will be situations where you may need to use plant-based protein sources: when you are unable to schedule prep time to take whole foods with you to work, to the gym, when traveling, or after working out when there is a short window of time (30 minutes to an hour post-workout) when you can quickly absorb amino acids from consumed protein sources.

Overall, plant-based protein powders are easily digestible, fight inflammation, and reduce muscle soreness more effectively than dairy-based protein powders. For best results either combine or look for a single protein powder that combines multiple sources of plant-based proteins.

Whey or casein protein is made from dairy (about 17-26g protein per 30g scoop) and is not plant-based and not recommended when transitioning to a plant-based diet.

Soy protein is plant-based but is highly processed and must be organic (see soy nutrition facts). If you choose this protein source, make sure the label reads, soy protein isolate.

My favorite protein powder brand is Billy's Protein Powder (vegan, organic, provides 18g protein/serving, hemp and brown rice protein blend, enzymes (optimizes protein absorption), nopal cactus

(sustains energy and speeds recovery), milk thistle (anti-inflammatory and liver support), arctic root (enhances stamina and vitality), vanilla, and stevia (sugar-free). This powder does not contain soy, whey, or sweeteners.

## PLANT-BASED PROTEIN POWDER PRODUCT CHART

| PRODUCT | NUTRITIONAL PROFILE |
|---|---|
| Hemp Protein Powder | 13-15g protein/2 tbsp, protein from edestin and albumin that are easily digestible, contains all amino acids (including 9 essential amino acids), specifically contains branch-chain amino acids (leucine, isoleucine and valine) that require less breakdown and more direct metabolism than other protein sources, safe plant source of protein without genetic modification (unlike soy protein-based powders), omega-6 essential fatty acids (inflammation-fighting), higher fiber content than other protein powders, compared to whey protein: similar calories, hemp contains about 4g heart-healthy unsaturated fat and fiber |
| Pea Protein Powder | 25g protein/30g scoop, contains all amino acids (including 9 essential amino acids), specifically contains branch-chain amino acids, contains three times more of the amino acid arginine (essential to building muscle) than whey protein and also particularly high in lysine, and phenylalanine, high in glutamic acid which helps convert carbs into energy so they won't be stored as fat |
| Brown Rice Protein Powder | 25-30g protein/scoop, does not contain all essential amino acids so combine with other plant-based proteins (some products also add in quinoa or chia proteins to compensate for amino acids rice protein lacks), faster absorption rate of the amino acid leucine as compared to whey protein, antioxidant properties, reduces glycemic response |

## Glossary and Frequently Asked Questions About Super Foods/Products Listed in This Section

**Vitamin B12** is a hot topic for people considering a plant-based lifestyle. Even though many think it is difficult to get enough of the vitamin if you don't consume animal products, actually it is quite easy.

*Vitamin B12 (cyanocobalamin)* is a water-soluble vitamin (excess intake is excreted in the urine) supporting the nervous system and formation of red blood cells. Vitamin B12 is not produced by animals or plants, but is produced by bacteria and fungi. Many animal foods contain higher amounts of B12 due to the fact that they accumulate bacteria throughout their lives and many receive this vitamin supplemented in their feed.

Vitamin B12 is less prominent today in plant foods with current soil conditions of increased pesticide and antibiotic concentrations, sanitizing practices in production of fermented foods, and bacterial control of air and water sources. You can get B12 from fortified foods like nut milks, cereals, and nutritional yeast, and in supplement form. This form of B12 in fortified foods is more readily absorbed in our gastrointestinal tract than the protein bound form found in animal products. In addition, consuming animal products has other negative health aspects such as increased levels of the hormone IGF-1 (associated with increased cancer risk and tumor growth) and other substances that cause injury to blood vessels promoting plaque formation.

Recommended Dietary Allowance (RDA) for Vitamin B12 is 2.4 mcg (micrograms) per day. If you are older than 50, you may have decreased absorption capacity and most of your intake should be through fortified foods or supplementation (non-protein bound form). Most cases of B12 deficiency are not due to inadequate intake, but to diminished absorption. Our bodies (some people better than others) efficiently recycle Vitamin B12 being reabsorbed in the intestine.

**Agave** is a sweetener/syrup made from the agave plant, 1.5 times sweeter than regular sugar, processing of agave strips the juice of all nutritional value with an end product that contains more fructose (up to 85%) than high fructose corn syrup. It is not recommended and good alternatives to agave include: honey, stevia, or dates.

**Cacao** (raw cacao or raw chocolate) can be found as a powder, cacao nibs, and raw cacao butter. Cacao is referred to as raw vegan chocolate from unroasted beans, minimally processed, with no additives.

**Selenium** is an essential mineral found in different concentrations in the soil and in certain plant-based foods such as Brazil nuts, sunflower seeds, chia seeds and mushrooms. Selenium has antioxidant effects that may help prevent chronic diseases, cardiovascular disease, cognitive decline, adequate levels ensure proper thyroid function, and immune system function which support its anti-cancer properties. Selenium is even more effective as an antioxidant when combined with Vitamin E.

**Goji Berries** have a unique flavor like a cross between a dried cherry, raisin, and cranberry. These berries contain more antioxidants than oranges, more Vitamin A than carrots, and more iron than soybeans and spinach. They also contain more than 20 vitamins and minerals.

**Tempeh** is made of fermented soybeans pressed into a block form that can be sliced and cubed for sautéing (producing a crisp golden crust) or baking. It is different from tofu in that it is made of the whole soybean and combined with the fermentation process it results in a higher protein, dietary fiber and vitamin profile. It is produced with only soybeans or a combination of beans and whole grains. It has a nutty flavor and can be eaten alone as a protein side-dish or mixed in a vegetable stir-fry or a protein topping on salads.

**Quinoa** (pronounced KEEN-wah) actually is not a grain but is a seed and a relative of the spinach family, beets and chard and is gluten free. Quinoa contains more vitamins, nutrients, and antioxidants than any other grain. It is a rich source of a complete protein, including lysine (not found in many other grains). Quinoa contains complex carbohydrates that digest slowly and reduce blood sugar spikes, is high in dietary fiber, and low in fat - exclusively made up of omega-3 fatty acids (healthy fats). Compared to brown rice, quinoa provides more dietary fiber and protein.

**Buckwheat Groats** are gluten free seeds from a plant related to rhubarb. The groats contain 6 grams of complete protein per ¼ cup, and are an excellent source of soluble and insoluble fiber. Can be used in any grain dish or as a breakfast hot porridge.

**Millet** is a gluten-free and often referred to as a grain due to its consistency, but it is actually a seed. It is rich in protein and essential amino acids, dietary fiber, B Vitamins, and is loaded with folate and choline, contains important minerals like magnesium, potassium, phosphorus, and zinc. Millet can be roasted, cooked like rice, or prepared for a creamy breakfast cereal.

**Wheat Germ** has a nutrient profile similar to flax seed. It contains fiber and 20% of your daily need of folic acid. Other nutrients include: magnesium, thiamin, phosphorus, and zinc.

**Sumac** is a tangy, lemony spice derived from the berries of the sumac bush that are dried and ground into powder. Great in dips and dressings.

**Algae products** are single-celled organisms and among the most nutritiously concentrated foods on earth, including the most potent source of complete protein of any food. They are packed with chlorophyll which results in an outstanding ability to detoxify and flush out heavy metals from the body including pesticides and environmental toxins. Other valuable properties of algae include the ability to alkalinize the body and enhance the immune system.

Two of the most popular algae products are **Chlorella and Spirulina**. Both have a strong, ocean-like taste, but you only need a small amount when added in powder form (also available in tablets). I personally love the flavor of chlorella and find it milder than spirulina. You will find one of my favorite snack recipes in this book featuring the combination of banana and chlorella. When sprinkled in your smoothie it not only provides you with nutrition off the charts but your drink will be a spectacular emerald green!

**Sea Vegetables** have ten times the mineral content of broccoli, and maca powder, good sources of iodine, calcium, and iron. Known for their ability to detoxify the body, studies indicate they provide protection against radiation (due to sodium alginate) and environmental pollutants. Anticancer and antitumoral properties. Great source of fluorine which is associated with support of the body's defenses and strengthens teeth and bones. There is practically no group of plants on the planet richer in nutrients, minerals, and trace minerals. Research indicates the health benefits are highest when consuming the seaweed raw.

The most commonly recognized form of sea vegetables are the sheets used in sushi **(Nori)**. **Dulse** is another variety of sea vegetable that is a dehydrated sea leaf that comes in powdered and flake forms. It can be sprinkled on salads, soups, and mixed in dressings. Prepare sea vegetables in sheet form by rinsing them, soaking in warm water until soft, rinse again and add to your salad or stir-fry at the end of cooking. If purchased in flake form, just sprinkle over salads, veggies, or soups. Very popular snacks that can be purchased in many grocery and gourmet stores are Roasted Seaweed Snacks which contain about 12 small sheets of salty seaweed. In the recipe snack section of the book you can get different ideas on how to make your own mini sushi snacks!

**Maca** has been used medicinally in the Peruvian Andes for thousands of years. It is a radish-like root, categorized as an "adaptagen." Maca has the ability to adjust/adapt to different stresses on the body dependent on the circumstance in order to balance the body. It provides energy and fights fatigue all while not being a stimulant. It is available in powder form and has a bit of a malty flavor when added to smoothies and desserts.

**Nutritional Yeast** is a deactivated yeast (not the same as Brewer's yeast) that is cultivated on molasses and is valuable in plant-based diets because it contains B vitamins, including B12. It comes in a powder and flake form and when added to dishes and dressings it adds a cheese-like flavor as well as provides nutritional benefits.

**Sucanat** is a whole unrefined cane sugar, minimally processed retaining its molasses content so can be used as a substitute for brown sugar. Use sparingly and not as part of the regular diet.

**Vanilla** is the only edible fruit of the orchid family. The time from picking the pods (beans) through curing (when beans turn dark brown) is about six months. Vanilla beans should be kept at room temperature in air-tight containers and not refrigerated (they develop mold when chilled). The vanilla bean contains thousands of tiny black seeds. Extract the seeds by slicing the bean down the middle and using the tip of a sharp knife, scrape the seeds from the interior of the bean. One inch or half of a vanilla bean is equal to one teaspoon of Pure Vanilla Extract (a cheaper form of vanilla). The cured vanilla beans are steeped in alcohol (must be 35 percent alcohol by volume according to FDA law) for Pure Vanilla Extract. Alcohol is the agent to extract flavor from the beans and since it is the carrier of flavor, the alcohol is burned off when vanilla is used in cooked foods. Non-alcoholic vanillas are usually labeled as Vanilla Flavor (not Pure Vanilla Extract per FDA requirements) and propylene glycol replaces alcohol as the extracting agent. Don't purchase Imitation Vanilla. Vanilla is the second most-expensive spice, after saffron.

### Egg Replacer Options:

- **Flax Egg** – 1 tbsp flaxmeal + 3 tbsp hot water
- **Ener-G Egg Replacer** (potato and tapioca starch) found in grocery stores, follow box instructions
- **Chia Egg** - 1 tbsp chia seeds + 3 tbsp hot water

### Product/Ingredient Resource Guide

| Company | Website |
| --- | --- |
| Navitas Naturals | www.navitasorganics.com |
| Ultimate Superfoods | www.ultimatesuperfoods.com |
| Billy's Infinity Greens | www.infinitygreens.com |
| Living Intentions | www.livingintentions.com |
| Amazon | www.amazon.com |

## Step Four: Library of Recipes for the 4-Month Plant-Based Conversion

I must confess, I am not an extravagant recipe developer/creator so don't feel badly if you aren't either! My focus, for you, is to provide you with meal plans that are nutritionally balanced, easy to prepare, offer versatile substitution options, and combine complimentary flavors that keep your taste buds happy. What I am good at is recognizing quality recipes from other plant-based gurus and I am sharing several of those with you in this section. I have added "Dena's Twists" (minor ingredient changes, superfood boosts, adding complimentary flavors). I also add detailed Food Prep techniques to save you time and ensure consistent results in the final product because some of the recipes were written for more people who may be further in their journey than you are, however, with my added notes, you too, can enjoy these amazing dishes.

Since this book is based on how I Fuel for Fitness, I'm sharing my favorite recipes with you. Some are my own while others are not. I identify where each recipe originated from at the beginning of a recipe and provide you with their websites, blogs, and social media contacts at the end of Step Four to save you time. As you lean into this new lifestyle, it is fun to discover new websites, new recipes and new ingredients. The contact information provided in this section will give you a head start on your adventure!

There are so many places to find full meal recipes from cookbooks to social media. The goal of this section is to provide you with one place to find delicious, easy recipes that will keep you on track with the plant-based lifestyle for at least four to five months. All of these recipes can be mixed, matched and rotated so there is no chance you will get bored.

Most of the recipes in the book are versatile and allow you the flexibility to substitute different vegetables or greens so don't dismiss a recipe if it highlights an ingredient that isn't your favorite. As you try the recipes, take note which dish/snack/dessert resonates with you with you the most and determine if it is due to fondness for the actual whole food, the sauce or dressing ingredients, or the texture of the finished product. Remember it is not a requirement to love every recipe just because it is plant-based. You will need to hone in on what ingredient and spice combinations you like the most. This will help you determine which new recipes to try in the future that you will place on your awesome "recipe keeper" list!

Plant-based recipes and menu building are very personal and individual. My personal style excludes vegan "processed" foods, imitation Western diet foods (e.g. vegan bacon, burgers), high fat condiments like vegan mayonnaise, and I have never been a big fan of breads, pasta (go figure, I am Italian!), or basic potatoes. In addition to nutritional and health reasons, I left behind meat and dairy because I didn't like the taste or texture of these foods, so I don't try to develop or share recipes that imitate those flavors. If you are a fan of these items, you won't find them in this book. There are however manufactured products out there for vegans that specifically mimic meat and even yam-based items that taste like and are shaped like shrimp! Many plant-based experts call these "transitional" vegan foods for folks that are just starting the process of leaning into the plant-based lifestyle. As you transition and try new things, you will develop your own individual style that works best for you.

When looking for new recipes, a great resource is social media where you will see beautiful photos and recipes of plant-based foods. Don't say I didn't warn you, but as you embrace this lifestyle, you will also be expanding your Instagram feed, your taste buds and naturally your pantry and superfood supplies. This is all positive and will support you living a healthy and quality life.

The recipe library in this book is categorized in the following way (the traditional lunch and dinner are not listed as a distinct section because the categorizes of Soups through Legumes can be interchanged for either of those meals providing for the widest variety of choices for meal planning/building):

**Breakfast Choices (22):**
Nut Milks
Dena's Power Nut/Seed Butter
Dena's Basic Green Smoothie
Nut Butter Green Smoothie
Green Citrus Smoothie
Green Cacao Smoothie
Strawberry Celery with Basil Smoothie
Banana Celery Cardamom Smoothie
Pear Goji Smoothie
Blueberry Banana Protein Smoothie
Oatmeal
Overnight Oats
Buckwheat Groats
Millet
Dena's Greens and Fruit Fusion
Chlorella Banana Bowl
Fruit Bowl Varieties with Nuts and Seeds
Pumpkin Apple Muffins
Wheatgerm Flax with Cranberry Muffins
Granola
Non-dairy Yogurt

**Snacks (13):**
Fresh fruit
Walnut-stuffed Medjool Dates
Rice Cakes with Toppings
Hemp Tahini Protein Blend
Seaweed Snacks with Toppings
Banana Slices with Tahini and Cacao Nibs
Chlorella Hemp Bars
Walnut and Seed Snack Bars
Almond Coconut Cranberry Energy Bars
Apricot Hemp Squares
Fig Banana Bowl
Cacao Pistachio Chia Bars
Citrus Fig Bars

**Dressings (15):**
Creamy Curry Dressing
Strawberry Hemp Dressing
Creamy Mustard Dressing
Hemp Seed Brazil Nut Power Dressing
Turmeric Tahini Dressing
Basil Parsley Dressing
Mango Red Pepper Dressing
Avocado Mango Pistachio Dressing

Mango Date Rosemary Dressing
Tahini Green Dressing
Liquid Gold Dressing
Cashew Chlorella Dill Dressing
Apple Curry Dressing
Orange Sesame Dressing
Asian Dressing

## Dips (15):

Lentil Cashew Dip
Pea and Edamame Guacamole Dip
Black Bean Cilantro Dip
Pinto Bean Basil Dip
Traditional Hummus
Cilantro Hummus
Sumac Hummus
Sun-Dried Tomato Hummus
Cauliflower Hummus
Broccoli Pea Blend
Macadamia and Sun-Dried Tomato Spread
Citrus Date Sesame Sauce
Cilantro Pesto with Olives
Parsley Basil Pesto
Pistachio Pesto

## Soups (5):

Grape Almond Soup
Pea Dill Soup with Seed Topping
Cauliflower Quinoa Hummus Soup
Carrot Curry Soup with Macadamia Nuts
Honeydew and Cucumber Soup

## Light Meals (10):

Roasted Vegetables
Roasted Broccoli with Tahini
Roasted Cauliflower with Tahini and Garlic
Roasted Beets with Orange and Dill
Steamed vegetables
Steamed Asparagus and Snow Peas
Boiled Vegetables
Raw Vegetables
Wraps (Green, Coconut) Zoodles
Sesame Oil Cucumber and Miso Mix

## Salads (4):

Papaya Avocado with Mixed Greens
Blueberry Beet and Walnut Salad
Cabbage Carrot Cucumber Slaw with Ginger Orange Tahini
Apricot Beet Salad with Apples and Cinnamon

## Legumes/Soy/Fermented Soy/Grains (8):

Tofu Scramble
Wheatberry Salad with Raisins
Farro with Red Pepper and Snow Peas
Ratatouille with Tofu
Asparagus Orange Quinoa with Pecans
Acorn Squash Stuffed with Cannellini Beans
Farro and Dried Cherries
Black Bean Enchiladas with Zucchini and Corn

## Desserts (8):

Cherry Chia Raw Crumble
Tahini Cashew Cacao Brownies
Cacao Walnut Hemp Seed Brownies
Salted Cashew Maca Tahini Squares
Garbanzo Protein Chocolate Cookies
Almond Date Balls Rolled in Coconut
Nanacream
Apple Raisin Pie

**Breakfast Choices**

I suggest starting the plant-based breakfast portion of the program by rotating items (see below) on your breakfast menu with a goal that by month two or three you will be consuming a "green" breakfast 3-4 times per week. This means either preparing a green smoothie, choosing to drink a green juice (purchased from a juice bar since we do not cover juicing as part of plant-based basics in this book), or consume my greens and fruit bowl (for maximum fiber and long-term hunger control) ultimately working your way to 5-6 times per week going "green" in the morning. In doing this, it not only moves you a step closer toward simplification in meal planning, preparation, and shopping, but it sets your daily foundation of maintaining nutritional balance in the plant-based lifestyle. Not only will you feel the difference in your energy throughout the day, but it will ensure you will get at least a minimum amount of "greens" into your system regardless of food availability or social obstacles you may face at lunch or dinner.

If you are not a breakfast person or you are an early morning work-out person and you are unable to fit in time for eating breakfast prior to getting to work or caring for children etc., these recipes are still valuable. One of the advantages of mastering these initial breakfast recipes is that they can also be utilized as one of your daily snacks or in combination with other low-calorie plant-based items of your choice when you are putting together a light lunch. Also remember that it's not all or nothing – some days you may have time for breakfast and some days you won't have time. This is another reason why it is so important to eat plant-based all day long so that if your schedule changes periodically or you miss a meal, you will always have the opportunity to meet your bodies nutritional needs at the next meal by following these plant-based guidelines.

Whenever we discuss healthy breakfast choices, the topic of juicing versus smoothies remains a hot topic. You will find advocates on both sides of the discussion. There are pros and cons to both liquid meals and whether you choose one or the other or indulge in both types of drinks will depend on your personal nutritional needs, health status, and the amount of produce you are consuming at other meals throughout the day.

Juicing extracts liquid from whole foods through a juicing machine (Centrifugal Juice Extractor or Masticating Juicer). Here are some of the pros and cons:

- Juicing maintains nutrients from the produce, but removes the fiber.
- Removing fiber also removes some nutrients.
- Juicing allows you to consume more greens that you may not ordinarily consume in their whole food form, either by direct juicing or by combining with fruit to sweeten the taste of the juice.
- The juicing process produces a drink with a higher concentration of sugar (caution for diabetics).
- Different types of juicers are better suited for vegetables versus fruits, but overall they require more produce than is used to produce a smoothie.
- Produce must be prepared, chopped, and slowly fed through the juicer for maximum efficiency.
- Juices have a thin, light texture and can be consumed easily.
- Juicers are time-consuming to clean .

Smoothies are made of whole fruits and vegetables combined in a high-speed blender. Here are some of the benefits:

- Blending maintains all of the nutrients from the produce, including fiber.
- Presence of fibers slows sugar absorption.
- Consumption of fiber promotes gut health.
- Presence of fiber and nutrients keeps you fuller longer than juices.
- It's easy to add supplements (protein powder) or other whole foods not easily juiced.
- Smoothies contain more calories than juices.

- Less produce is  required to make a single smoothie versus a juice serving.

- It's faster to make a smoothie versus a juice.

- Blending produces a thick texture that can also be served cold by adding ice to the blender.

- Blenders are a quick clean up.

The reason I have not included juicing as part of this book is that it really is a science in itself and I believe it is not essential to people just starting to embrace the plant-based lifestyle. You need to research the different types of juicers, match that with the types of juices you plan to make, and be ready to make a substantial investment in the equipment. If you are interested in incorporating juicing, I will provide you with resources at the end of this section for recipes from expert juice gurus for your review.

For me personally, I juiced daily for many years and the rapid concentrated delivery was overpowering for my body. It did not sustain my needs as an athlete and I had problems with bloating. However, I do enjoy juicing occasionally and use juices like carrot and beet in soup recipes. I now enjoy smoothies as a post-workout refuel opportunity and also make my own nut milk to add to the blender of whole foods.

I have replaced my morning juice with eating a bowl of greens and fruit rather than juicing or having a smoothie. This works better for me to sustain me throughout the morning, and it still allows me to get my morning greens while mixing in a generous amount of nuts and seeds for extra protein. I share my bowl of greens recipes in this section for you to try. Remember this is what works for my body, you may discover that you feel best when you juice versus consuming smoothies or you can't eat a bowl of greens for breakfast and smoothies work better for you. This is part of the adventure with plant-based living, you are able to customize your meals and snacks for what works for you. This exercise of discovery actually makes you more aware of your body, its unique needs, and what fuel is right for you.

Now let's start out with some of these breakfast options! Here are two basic recipes that can be breakfast items on their own, part of other breakfast recipes, or will be part of snack and/or dessert recipes listed later in this book.

### Nut Milks—Standard Nut Milk

- **1 cup of nuts (almonds, cashews, hazelnuts, Brazil nuts)**
- **2 ½ -3 cups filtered water**
- **Pinch of sea salt**
- **Optional sweeteners: 1-2 tbsp of maple syrup, honey, or coconut sugar, or 2 pre-soaked medjool dates**

1. Soak nuts overnight (cashews require only 4 hours).
2. Prior to adding to a high-speed blender, drain nuts, and rinse a final time.
3. Blend nuts (without soak water) with filtered water until the mixture is creamy.
4. Drape a milk bag over a large container / mason jar (for storage of milk in refrigerator), and pour milk from blender into bag.
5. Pull drawstring to close bag, lift bag above jar, and twist bag with your hands to squeeze out milk into jar while retaining any solid particulates in the bag.
6. Put lid on jar or cover container and store milk in the refrigerator for 6-7 days.

### Flavored Nut Milks

Follow Standard Nut Milk recipe, but before blending, add the ingredients shown below.

**For Vanilla Cardamom Nut Milk:**

- **2 tsp vanilla, ½ tbsp cardamom**
- **several dates or 2 tbsp honey**

**For Cacao Nut Milk:**

- **1 tbsp cacao powder**
- **several dates or 2 tbsp honey**

### Dena's Power Nut/Seed Butter

- **1 cup seed mixture (1/3 each pumpkin, hemp, and sunflower seeds)**
- **1 cup nut mixture (either half cup each of cashew and almond, or 1/3 cup each cashew and almond, with the last third your choice of walnuts, pistachios, or pecans) or go totally decadent and add Macadamia nuts.**
- **¾ tsp sea salt (If you don't want any salt, exclude this ingredient.)**

1. Place all ingredients in the food processor and let it run for 12-15 minutes. As the nuts and seeds heat up they will release their oils and start to become creamy.
2. During the processing time you will have to stop the processor multiple times, use a spatula to scrape down the sides and floor of the unit, and then start her back up again.
3. You will know it's done when the mixture is creamy and has the texture of nut butter.
4. Store in a glass container in the refrigerator for up to one month. It generally doesn't last in my kitchen for more than 5 days – it's that good…

### Green Smoothies

**(Smoothies also make great mid-day snacks)**

If you would like to transform the smoothie recipes to a breakfast bowl (a thicker version of a smoothie you can eat in a bowl with a spoon), just reduce the liquid content (which will result in a thicker end product), scoop into a bowl, and add toppings like shredded coconut, chopped apples, dried fruit, cacao nibs, and/or sprinkle with chia seeds, cinnamon, or cacao powder.

### Dena's Basic Green Smoothie

- 1 1/2 cups nut milk
- 1 1/4 cup blueberries (fresh or frozen)
- 2 cups greens (kale, romaine, spinach)
- 1-2 small bananas (fresh or frozen)
- 1 tbsp flaxseed meal
- 1 tbsp chlorella
- 1 tsp vanilla
- 2 tsp cinnamon
- 1 scoop (1-2 tbsp) vegan protein powder

1. Combine all ingredients in the order listed into a blender, add ice (1 cup) if desired, and blend. Sprinkle cacao nibs on top.
2. Customize this smoothie recipe by changing the greens, spices (consider clove, nutmeg, pumpkin pie spice), and berries.

### Nut Butter Green Smoothie

**(One of my favorite recipes inspired by Julie Morris, Superfood Smoothies with Dena's Twist and Food Prep Tips)**

- 1 1/2 cup nut milk (use a vanilla flavor)
- 2 tbsp Dena's nut butter
- 2/3 cup celery, chopped
- 1/3 cup dried mulberries
- 2 cups spinach
- 3 tbsp vegan protein powder
- 1-2 medjool dates (desired sweetness)

1. Make Dena's Power Nut/Seed Butter (found at the beginning of the Breakfast Recipe section).
2. Combine all ingredients in the order listed into a blender, add ice (1 cup) if desired, and blend.
3. Options: Trade out protein powder for hemp seeds, and trade out mulberries for dried cranberries.

### Green Smoothie Variation—Green Citrus Smoothie

**(One of my favorite recipes inspired by Julie Morris, Superfood Smoothies with Dena's Twist and Food Prep Tips)**

- 1 1/2 cups orange juice
- 1 1/2 tsp orange zest
- 1/2 cup cashews
- 1/4 cup mulberries
- 2 tsp fresh rosemary
- 1/2 tsp sumac
- 3 cup mixture of spinach and chard
- 1 medjool date

1. Wash 1-2 oranges, use the microplane to zest (remove the rind), and set aside the zest.
2. Cut the orange(s) in half and juice with citrus juicer.
3. Combine all ingredients in the order listed into a blender, add ice (1 cup) if desired, and blend.

### Green Smoothie Variation—Green Cacao Smoothie

**(One of my favorite recipes adapted from Julie Morris, Superfood Smoothies with Dena's Twist and Food Prep Tips)**

- 1 1/2 cups nut milk (try hemp or cashew or go decadent with macadamia nut)
- 2 tbsp hemp seeds
  2 tbsp cacao powder
- 3 tbsp cacao nibs
- 1 tbsp cardamom
- 2 frozen chopped bananas (check *Step Seven, Common Food Prep Technique Tips— Determining When Bananas Are Ripe and Storage:*)
- 1 cup each chopped kale and romaine
- 1-2 medjool dates

Combine all ingredients in the order listed into a blender, add ice (1 cup) if desired, and blend.

- 1/4 cup of water
- **Ice cubes (handful) if desired**

Combine all ingredients in the order listed into a blender, add ice (1 cup) if desired, and blend.

**Strawberry Celery with Basil Smoothie**

- **1 cup fresh strawberries, sliced**
- **1 cup celery, chopped**
- **1/2 banana**
- **1/4 cup fresh basil, chopped**
- **3-4 medjool dates**
- **1/8-1/4 cup Brazil nuts**
- **1 tbsp lemon juice**

*• add 1 cup almond milk*

**Banana Celery Cardamom Smoothie**

**(One of my favorite recipes by Cherie Soria, Brenda Davis, R.D., & Vesanto Melina, M.S., R.D., in "The Raw Food Revolution Diet"— post-workout refueling of electrolytes with potassium from bananas and sodium from celery)**

- **4 ripe bananas, sliced**
- **2-3 celery stalks, chopped**
- **1/2 tbsp cardamom**
- **Add small amount of water if needed to blend**

Combine all ingredients in the order listed into a blender, add ice (1 cup) if desired, and blend. See photo on page 40 (top left) and note on page 46.

## Pear Goji Smoothie

(One of my favorite recipes inspired by Julie Morris, Superfood Smoothies with Dena's Twist and Food Prep Tips)

- 1 1/4 cups almond milk
- 1/3 cup goji berries
- 2 medjool dates
- 1/4 inch knob of fresh ginger
- 2 tsp cinnamon
- 2 pears, chopped
- 2 cups fresh spinach

1. Allow goji berries to soften in almond milk in Vitamix while peeling ginger and chopping dates and pears.
2. Blend all ingredients in the order listed in a Vitamix. Then add ice (1 cup) if desired, and blend.

## Blueberry Banana Protein Smoothie

- 2 cups almond or hemp milk
- 2-3 medium-sized ripe bananas (can be frozen)
- 1/2 cup blueberries (fresh or frozen)
- 1-2 tbsp protein powder
- 1 tsp maca powder
- 1-2 tsp cardamom

Blend all ingredients in the order listed in a Vitamix. Then add ice (1 cup) if fruit isn't frozen, blend, and enjoy!

## Smoothie Nutritional Bomb Supplements—High Nutrition Enhancements

Add the following to smoothies to enhance taste and better meet your nutritional needs:

- Protein powder
- Chlorella
- Flaxseed meal, chia seeds, hemp seed
- Avocado
- Goji berries
- Nuts or nut butter/tahini
- Cinnamon, turmeric, and/or ginger
- Maca powder
- Cacao powder, cacao nibs
- Shredded coconut

**Grains: Oatmeal, Overnight Oats, Buckwheat Groats, and Millet**

**Oatmeal**—five types from least to most processed, from highest (keeps you fuller longer) to lowest fiber content:

1. **Steel-cut oats (Irish oats)**—minimal processing, take the longest to cook, chewy texture, high fiber and protein
2. **Scottish oats**—minimal processing, slight decrease in fiber and protein, less chewy than steel-cut
3. **Rolled oats (Old fashioned)**—cook faster than steel-cut oats and commonly used in baked goods, digested faster than steel-cut oats with a higher spike in blood sugar
4. **Quick oats**—the most processed of the top four oatmeal varieties, cooks up quickly, mushy texture, higher glycemic index
5. **Instant**—most processed, lowest fiber, highest glycemic index, usually pre-flavored with added sugar

**Overnight oats**—No cook method for preparing oatmeal using rolled oats due to their ability to quickly soak up whatever liquid is used for soaking...

**Traditional overnight oats basics:**

- 1/3 cup non-dairy yogurt
- 1/2 cup rolled oats
- 2/3 cup nut milk
- 1 tbsp flaxseed meal or chia seeds
- 1/2 tsp vanilla
- 1/2 tsp cinnamon
- 0-1 tbsp sweetener (honey or maple syrup) or 1/2 a ripe banana, mashed.

1. Mix oats with liquid and other customized ingredients in a bowl.
2. Spoon mixture into a mason jar and cover with lid.
3. Refrigerate overnight, ready to go in the morning with a creamy delicacy.
4. **Customize with add-ins and toppings:** nut butter, cacao powder, chopped fresh fruit, dried fruit, shredded coconut, spices.

You can store overnight oats in the refrigerator for 3-5 days, so you can incorporate making overnight oats in advance in your Sunday meal prep schedule for breakfast and/or snacks.

**Buckwheat groats**—gluten-free, termed a pseudocereal, but actually a fruit seed, a high-quality protein containing all essential amino acids. To prepare:

1. Soak 1 cup of groats to reduce cooking time. (See soaking directions in Step Two, Legumes/Soy/Fermented Soy/Grains Food Chart.)

2. Rinse thoroughly.

3. Dry-toast the groats in a pan for 2-3 minutes on medium heat while stirring.

4. Then add 2 1⁄2 cups non-dairy milk, spices (cinnamon, nutmeg, clove), and a pinch of salt.

5. Cover and simmer until water is absorbed (about 10 minutes).

6. Use similar add-ins and toppings as for oatmeal, plus sweeteners if desired.

The thick and chewy texture stands up well to reheating, so make in large batches to have ready-made groats for several days.

**Millet**—a small-seeded grass with significant amounts of protein and fiber, as well as B-vitamins, calcium potassium, magnesium, and iron. To prepare:

- **1/3 cup millet rinsed and drained**
- **1/2 cup non-dairy milk**
- **3/4 cup of water**
- **Spices of choice (cinnamon, pumpkin pie spice, nutmeg, clove)**
- **1 tsp vanilla**
- **Sprinkle of salt.**

Place ingredients in a saucepan, bring initially to a boil, then turn down to simmer, and cover for 20-25 minutes. Add sweetener and toppings as desired.

**Pictured at right: Millet with chia, blueberries, and pistachios**

### Dena's Greens and Fruit Fusion (my daily breakfast/lunch)

- **2-3 cups chopped greens (romaine, kale, spinach, mustard greens, chard)**
- **1 stalk of celery, chopped**
- **3/4 of an apple (Fuji is best), chopped**
- **1/4 cup of blueberries**
- **Handful of raisins or cranberries, chopped**
- **1/2 of an orange, juiced**
- **2 tbsp flaxmeal**
- **1 tbsp chia seeds**
- **1/2 tbsp chlorella**
- **1/2 tbsp cinnamon**
- **1/2 tbsp turmeric**
- **Sprinkle of clove**
- **Sprinkle of pepper**
- **Pumpkin seeds, walnuts, and cacao nibs to sprinkle on top**

1. Wash greens and dry them in salad spinner.

2. Chop apple and celery, and add blueberries and dried fruit, all to medium-sized bowl.

3. Juice the orange directly over the bowl.

4. Add the ingredients flaxmeal through pepper, and carefully mix all ingredients.

5. Take greens out of spinner and finely chop. Then add to bowl of fruit, give a final mix, and top with seeds, nuts, and cacao nibs.

**Variations of this recipe:** Change the greens and fruit dependent on what is in season.

4. Once combined, slowly blend in chlorella (add in small increments).

5. Refrigerate overnight, and enjoy the next morning with your choice of toppings: coconut, seeds, dried fruit. This is also a great post-workout snack.

### Chlorella Banana Bowl

**(One of my favorite recipes inspired by Susan Voisin, fatfreevegan.com)**

- 1 tbsp chia seeds
- 1/2 cup nut milk (almond or cashew)
- 1/4 tsp honey or more for desired sweetness (optional)
- 1 ripe banana, mashed
- 1/2 tsp cardamom
- 1 tbsp chlorella
- Toppings: coconut, seeds, dried fruit

1. In a small bowl, combine chia, milk, honey (if using), and cardamom. Set aside for 5 minutes to thicken.

2. Place banana on a small plate and mash with a fork until creamy.

3. Stir chia mixture to ensure it's well combined and thick, then add banana mash and mix.

### Fruit Bowl with Nuts and Seeds

Any combination of fruits topped with nuts or seeds can be a healthy and speedy light breakfast. Fruit on its own or in pairings can also serve as snacks or a dessert option. I have listed below some of my favorite mixes, but I personally feel pumpkin seeds can be sprinkled on any fruit—but that's just me! Try some of these combinations and start pairing some of your own.

- **Apple with raisins and pecans, sprinkled with pumpkin pie spice**
- **Apple and medjool dates with pumpkin seeds**
  **Apple and banana with dried tart cherries**
  **Apples, oranges, dried cranberries**
- **Banana with papaya and chopped macadamia nuts**
- **Drizzle tahini over banana slices and sprinkle with cacao nibs**
- **Banana with sunflower seed butter**

- Banana slices drizzled with melted dark chocolate
- Banana with dried figs and pistachios
- Strawberries and bananas, sprinkled with cinnamon
- Drizzle balsamic vinegar over strawberries, then sprinkle with coconut sugar and a dash of pepper
- Strawberries with walnuts and chopped mint
- Strawberry, kiwi, dried cranberries
- Strawberries drizzled with melted dark chocolate
- Mango with banana
- Mango with raspberries
- Mango with strawberries and pumpkin seeds
- Tangerines and apples sprinkled with hemp seeds
- Peaches, kiwi, and blackberries
- Pears and raspberries
- Pear, peach, dried cranberries with walnuts
- Apricot and Cherries with pistachios
- Cantaloupe, apple, raspberries or goji berries
- Grapes with chopped almonds
- Raspberries with dried cranberries
- Honeydew melon with blueberries and pistachios
- Grape, orange, and kiwi with pumpkin seeds

1. Chop fruit in bite-sized pieces, place in a bowl, and sprinkle with add-ons or mix-ins. (This can be nuts / seeds, coconut, cacao nibs, fresh berries or dried fruits.)

2. If preparing fruit bowls for the next morning, chop fruit, place it in a glass container, and store it in the refrigerator overnight. If adding nuts and seeds, store them in a separate container and add to the fruit just prior to enjoying your fruit bowl.

**Bakery Items—Muffins**

**Pumpkin Apple Muffins (makes 14-16 muffins)**

- **2 apples, peeled, chopped—plain or roasted. (If roasted, see below for directions.)**
- **1 1/2 cup flour (any except standard white flour)**
- **1/2 cup coconut sugar**
- **1/2 cup sucanat**
- **2 tsp pumpkin pie spice**
- **1 tsp baking soda**
- **1/4 tsp baking powder**
- **1/4 tsp salt**
- **1 cup canned pumpkin**
- **1/2 cup nutmilk (almond, hemp, etc.) Egg replacer = 1 egg**
- **1/4 cup grapeseed oil**
- **1/4 cup applesauce**

**To roast apples (optional):**

1. Preheat oven to 350°.
   Place peeled,
   chopped apples in a medium bowl. Sprinkle with 1 tbsp cinnamon and 1 tbsp sweetener (either agave or maple syrup).
2. Stir to coat apples, place them in oiled baking dish, and put them into oven for 30 minutes.
3. Use as needed in recipe, and refrigerate extra sauce for snacking.

**To make muffins:**

1. Place apples in processor and make apple sauce.
2. Preheat oven to 375°.
3. Prepare your egg replacer (see options below).
4. Place prepared paper muffin cups into muffin baking pan.
5. Get a large bowl, combine all dry ingredients through salt, and stir with a whisk.
6. Combine remaining ingredients in a medium bowl and stir with a whisk.
7. Add pumpkin mixture to the large bowl of dry ingredients and mix with a spatula, folding just to combine ingredients.

8. Fill about 14-16 muffin cups 3/4 full.
9. Bake for 20 minutes. Check if done by inserting a toothpick in the center of a muffin. Muffins are done if toothpick comes out without any uncooked batter sticking to it.
10. Cool muffins for 5 minutes, then remove from pan.

**Wheatgerm and Flax with Cranberry Muffins (Recipe makes about one dozen muffins.)**

- 1 tbsp grated orange zest (1-2 oranges)
- 1/2 cup orange juice (about 1 orange juiced)
- Egg replacer (1 tsp replacer + 2 tbsp water)
- 1 1/2 cup flour (any except standard white flour)
- 1/4 cup raw wheat germ
- 1/4 cup flaxseed meal
- 1/2 tsp baking soda
- 1 tsp cinnamon
- 1/4 tsp nutmeg
- 1/4 tsp sea salt
- 3/4 cup sucanat
- 1/4 cup grapeseed oil
- 1/2 cup dried cranberries
- 1 tbsp sucanat for sprinkling

1. Preheat oven to 375°.
   Prior to mixing ingredients, prepare the following: Wash 1-2 oranges, use the microplane to zest (remove the rind), and set aside zest.
2. Cut the orange(s) in half and juice with citrus juicer.
3. Mix egg replacer with water and set aside. Place oiled paper muffin cups into muffin baking pan.
4. Combine all dry ingredients (flour through salt) in a large bowl and mix with a whisk.
5. Combine sucanat, oil, zest, juice, and egg replacer in a small bowl and mix with a whisk.
6. Add orange juice mixture to dry mixture and mix with a spatula, just to combine.

7. Spoon batter ¾ full into prepared muffin cups.
8. Sprinkle tops of each muffin with sucanat.
9. Bake for 17 minutes. Check if done by inserting a toothpick in the center of a muffin. Muffins are done if toothpick comes out without any uncooked batter sticking to it.

Did you know?: There are endless combinations for nutritious, brightly colored smoothies. Start adding your favorite ingredients and post your masterpiece on social media.

Banana Celery Cardamom Smoothie (page 39)—Cardamom is a member of the ginger family with a unique flavor and aroma described as floral, citrus, and even smoky.

Cardamom has flavor compounds in common with rosemary. I was introduced to cardamom by my Swedish aunt who made a cardamom cake that became one of my favorite desserts as a kid, and I incorporate the spice into many of my plant-based recipes as my form of "comfort food."

Grains, Millet (page 42) —Those of you who are bird lovers will recognize millet as a favorite seed treat for birds that is nutritious, low in fat, and aids in digestion. Birds love to pick millet off the stalk (spray millet) due to its texture, delicate taste, and to satisfy foraging needs. Celebrating the multi-species love of millet...

Bakery Items, Muffins—The term "prepared" muffin tins in a recipe means lightly coating the muffin pan with coconut oil or other high melting point oil or a spray oil (for ease of application) if placing batter directly into the muffin tin. If using paper muffin liners inserted into the muffin pan, follow the same process of lightly coating the paper liner. Using paper liners makes muffin pan clean up a lot faster without cooked batter sticking to the pan.

Plant-based Store-bought Items, Non-dairy Yogurt—Food labels on milk-based yogurt only tell you total sugar, which includes the naturally occurring sugar or lactose in the yogurt. With non-dairy yogurts, there is no sugar from lactose, but many products add berries or other fruits that increase the sugar content. To determine the added sugar in regular yogurt, subtract 15-16 grams of lactose (average natural sugar in yogurt) per 1 cup serving, which leaves the added sugar content. Greek yogurt averages 6-9 grams of lactose per 1 cup serving (also less calcium than regular yogurt). Studies show the added sugar in one cup serving of milk-based yogurt ranges between 10 to 30 grams (depending on the brand). This added sugar is from fruit (fruit on the bottom, fruit flavored), sweeteners (evaporated cane syrup, fruit juice concentrate, cane sugar), and toppings.

**Did you know?: While you are becoming more familiar with portion sizes and calorie counts, it is a good idea to start out with pre-measured sizes of homemade nut/seed snack bags and trail mixes. A one-ounce portion of nuts (about a handful) provides between 128-204 calories depending on the type of nut. The top three highest caloric nuts in a one ounce serving include:**

1. **Macadamia nuts (204 calories)**
2. **Pecans (196 calories)**
3. **Pine Nuts (191 calories).**

**The top three highest caloric seeds in a one ounce serving include:**

1. **Sunflower Seeds (165 calories)**
2. **Pumpkin Seeds (163 calories)**
3. **Hemp Seeds (157 calories).**

**Try to start out at ¼ cup daily, and dependent on your overall daily caloric intake, you can work your way up to a ½ cup combination of nuts and seeds, dependent on your desire to lose or maintain weight.**

### Plant-based Store-bought Items

**Granola/Cereal**—I rarely eat cereal but if I am traveling or need a snack, I enjoy Living Intentions vegan, gluten-free, sprouted varieties: **Blueberry Blast** and **Banana Hemp.**

**Nut Butter** is easy to make at home (Dena's Power Nut/Seed Butter), but if you want to buy it, look for raw varieties, low in sugar.

**Nut Milk** comes in many varieties including: almond, hemp, cashew, and macadamia. Try to find unsweetened varieties with low sugar content. Best choice, follow the home-made recipe at the beginning of the Breakfast section.

**Non-dairy yogurt** is available in soy, nut milk, and coconut varieties, check sugar levels in these products.

**Tahini** is sesame seeds in paste form, rich in minerals and Vitamins B and E, more protein than most nuts and dairy milk. Use in salad dressings, dips, in place of nut butters.

### Resource Guide for More Information on Juicing and Smoothies:

- "Superfood Smoothies," by Julie Morris (100 Delicious, Energizing & Nutrient Dense Recipes)
- John the Juicer (John Kohler), Choosing the right juicer, with John Kohler (YouTube—Health Forward)
- Discountjuicers.com
- Steve Prussack – http://juiceguru.com
- http://JustJuice.org

### Snack Choices

Plant-based snacks provide an opportunity to build upon the healthy, essential nutrients you are consuming during meals. Because life isn't always timed perfectly, you may have to work late, or the kid's soccer game may go longer than expected, or you may just spend an extra hour in traffic on the way home so your standard dinner meal time is now off schedule. These are moments when you may need to reach for "fuel" for your body to sustain your energy levels until you can consume a planned plant-based meal. For those of you who are exercising (regular

fitness is essential to maximize the benefits of a plant-based lifestyle), you will need snacks that support your recovery from exercise. Just as you plan your workout time, you should also be planning your snacks pre- and post-workout, to help enhance your performance.

Individual snacks or a combination of snacks should try to achieve delivering a protein source, some carbohydrate, and fiber to keep you fuller longer, and let's not forget terrific flavor! Plant-based proteins in snacks vary from nuts, to seeds like hempseeds, and non-dairy protein-powders. I promote bananas in snacks, not only for carbohydrate benefits (pack more carbs per bite than other fruits due to low water content), but for the potassium replacement associated with post-workout muscle maintenance, and a variety of dried fruits such as dates, figs, and apricots which provide fiber.

Most of the snacks in the recipe library can easily be frozen and taken out as you need them, for example, taking them with you to work or having them available in your gym bag after a workout. I have also tested these snacks on kids from elementary school age through high school, and I can happily report that they are popular in these age groups as well!

As discussed in *Breakfast Choices*, you can easily whip up a plant-based smoothie that also fulfills your snack nutritional needs, and Dena's Power Nut/Seed Butter (both recipes can be found in *Breakfast Choices*) can stand alone as a snack spread on fruit and/or serves as an ingredient in some of the snack recipes in this section.

### Fast Easy Snacks

Glycemic Index (GI) is a number assigned to a food based on how fast your body converts the carbohydrates from the food into glucose. The lower the GI, the less the food impacts your blood sugar. A low (good) GI = 55 or less, medium GI = 56-69, high GI = 70 or higher. The lower GI helps you determine "good carbs" which are more slowly digested. However, the GI of a food can change under different conditions. For example, as fruits ripen (like bananas), the GI will increase. When you consume a meal, the overall GI can be lowered if it contains more low-glycemic items on the plate than high-glycemic items.

**Fruit is a carbohydrate,** and certain fruits have a low GI. Starting with the lowest GI score: cherries, grapefruits, apples, pears, strawberries, peaches, and oranges. Fruit can be a great snack on its own and can help contribute to increasing your daily intake of fruit. When protein (nuts and seeds, nut butters, tahini) is combined with a fruit , it creates a longer lasting energy snack. See the fruit recipes in the *Breakfast* section and in this section.

**Dr. Dena and Jackson enjoying homemade coconut yogurt with granola at our favorite Southern California vegan eatery...**

### Walnut-stuffed Medjool Dates (next page #1)

- **4-5 pitted medjool dates, sliced in half**
- **Handful of chopped walnuts**

1. Arrange 8-10 medjool date halves on a plate.
2. Fill the center of each date equally with walnuts. Enjoy!

### Rice Cakes with Toppings (next page #2)

1. Slice avocado in half, remove pit, spoon out the fruit, and spread on rice cakes.
2. Drizzle or spray Bragg's Liquid Aminos or Coconut Aminos on cakes.
3. Topping Options:
   - Nut Butters
   - Macadamia Nut & Sun-Dried Tomato Dip
   - Edamame & Pea Guacamole
   - Hummus.
4. Be creative and explore your own flavor combinations!

### Hemp Tahini Protein Blend (next page #3)

1. In a small bowl, use a fork to blend half of a small avocado, 1-2 tbsp tahini, and 1 tbsp hemp seeds until creamy.
2. Mix in goji berries and cacao nibs (dulse flakes optional).
3. Eat straight up or spread on crackers, apples, or rice cakes.

### Seaweed Snacks with Toppings (next page #4)

- Avocado, hemp seeds sprinkled with Bragg's or Tamari
- Avocado and sprouts
- Hummus or other vegan dips

### Banana Slices with Tahini and Cacao Nibs

1. Chop ripe banana into bite-sized slices.
2. Place in a bowl, drizzle with tahini, and top with cacao nibs.
3. For variations, switch out tahini for various nut butters.

EDAMAME & PEA GUACAMOLE

#1

#2

#3

#4

#5

### Chlorella Hemp Bars (Raw)

(Based on a great recipe adapted from Vegetarian Times Magazine, June 2016 with Dena's Twist and Food Prep Tips)

- 1 tbsp grated lemon zest
- 3/4 cup raw almonds
- 1 cup medjool dates, chopped
- 3 tbsp vegan protein powder
- 1 tsp chlorella
- 1 tbsp lemon juice
- 1/2 cup hemp seeds
- 1/2 cup shredded coconut

1. Place parchment paper on a cutting board, set aside.
2. Wash/scrub 1-2 lemons (depending on size), and using a microplane, zest lemons to equal 1 tbsp zest.
3. Place almonds in the processor and grind into small crumbs (leaving a small amount of texture).
4. Add dates to the processor along with protein powder, chlorella, lemon juice, and zest, mixing until mixture forms a ball and sticks together easily.
5. Carefully redistribute the mixture evenly in the processor. Then add hemp seeds and coconut and use the pulse button to combine without completely chopping.
6. Pull mixture out of processor and place on parchment papered cutting board.
7. Using your hands, flatten into a 1⁄2-inch-thick rectangle. Cut into bars or small squares. (Store in the refrigerator or freezer.)

### Walnut and Seed Snack Bars (Raw—at left, #5)

(Based on a great recipe adapted from Emily Voneuw, of Thisrawsomeveganlife.com with Dena's Twist and Food Prep Tips)

- 1 cup medjool dates, chopped and set aside
- 1 cup walnuts
- 1/3 cup chia seeds
- 1/3 cup flaxseeds, ground
- 1/3 cup hemp seeds
- 3/4 cup pumpkin seeds
- 1/4 cup cacao nibs
- 1/4 cup shredded coconut
- 1/2 cup yellow raisins

1. Chop dates and set aside.
2. Set aside a small amount of all ingredients (except dates and raisins) in a small bowl.
3. Use processor to chop walnuts into large chunks, add remaining ingredients (except dates and raisins), and coarsely blend.
4. Add dates and raisins, and process until mixture forms a ball.
5. Remove mixture, place it in a bowl and hand-mix in unprocessed nuts/seeds that were set aside earlier.
6. Line a loaf pan with parchment paper, evenly press mixture in pan using your hands, and with a sharp knife cut into bars or squares.
7. Refrigerate for 1-2 hours to harden. (Store in the refrigerator or freezer.)

### Fig Banana Bowl (The Raw Food Revolution Diet)

(One of my favorite recipes by Cherie Soria, Brenda Davis, R.D., & Vesanto Melina M.S., R.D. , in "The Raw Food Revolution Diet")

- 3 large, very ripe bananas chopped in bite-sized pieces
- 12 large dried figs, soaked for 30 minutes to 1 hour (reserve soak water)
- 2 tsp cinnamon
- 1 tsp cardamom

Place all ingredients in a Vitamix in the order listed and blend until smooth. If needed, add very small amount of fig soak water just to support the blending process while keeping the mixture thick. (Eat immediately or store in the refrigerator or freezer. The puree will thicken over time.)

## Almond Coconut Cranberry Energy Bars (Raw)

- 1 cup raw almonds
- 1 1/2 cup medjool dates, chopped
- 1/2 cup dried cranberries
- 1/2 cup shredded coconut
- 1 tbsp vanilla

1. Place parchment paper on a cutting board and set aside.
2. Place almonds in processor and chop into small pieces.
3. Add chopped dates, spreading evenly in the processor, and combine to a creamy mixture.
4. Add remaining ingredients and pulse to maintain texture.
5. Place on parchment-covered cutting board, and using your hands, shape into a 1/2-inch-thick rectangle and cut into bars or squares. Store in refrigerator or freezer (will last 2 weeks).

## Apricot Hemp Squares (Raw—see near right)

**(Based on a great recipe adapted from wholefoodsmarket.com with Dena's Twist and Food Prep Tips)**

- 3 cups dried apricots
- 1 cup medjool dates, chopped
- 1 cup hempseeds
- 2 tbsp lemon juice
- 1 tsp ground nutmeg
- 1 tsp vanilla

1. Line an 8 X 8 pan with parchment paper.
2. Roughly chop the apricots and set aside.
3. Chop dates and process until smooth.
4. Add apricots and remaining ingredients, and process into a chunky paste.
5. Press mixture evenly into pan using
6. your fingers and refrigerate at least 2 hours until paste becomes firm.
7. Then cut into squares. Store in refrigerator or freezer.

## Cacao Pistachio Chia Bars

**(Based on a great recipe adapted from Vegetarian Times Magazine, January 2010, with Dena's Food Prep Tips)**

- 1 cup pistachios
- 1 3/4 cup chopped medjool dates
- 1/3 cup cacao powder
- 1/3 cup chia seeds
- 1/2 tsp vanilla

1. Add pistachios to processor and chop, leaving some texture. Then set aside.
2. Place dates in processor and chop until mixture is creamy.
3. Add remaining ingredients except pistachios, and process until well combined.
4. Add pistachios and pulse until just combined.
5. Place mixture on a parchment-covered cutting board. Using fingers, shape into a 1/2-inch-thick rectangle and cut into bars or squares.
6. Refrigerate 1-2 hours. (Store in refrigerator or freezer.)

## Citrus Fig Bars (Raw)

**(Based on a great recipe adapted from Christine Bailey in "The Raw Food Healing Bible" with Dena's Food Prep Tips)**

**Filling:**
- 5 oz dried figs soaked in water for 1 hour
- 1 tsp orange or lemon zest (or combination)
- 2 tsp orange juice

**Cookie Crust:**
- 1 1/3 cup almonds
- 1/3 cup macadamia nuts
- 3/4 cup pecans
- 1/4 cup shredded coconut
- 1/3 cup flaxseed, ground
- 5 oz medjool dates
- 1 tbsp orange juice
- 1 tsp cinnamon

- **1/2 tsp clove**
- **1/2 tsp vanilla**

1. Soak figs for at least 1 hour.
2. Zest orange/lemon, then juice, and set aside.
3. Drain figs, place in a processor with remaining filling ingredients, mix into a creamy paste (puree), and place in a small bowl.
4. Chop dates and set aside.
5. Place nuts, coconut, and flaxseed in the processor and mix to size of crumbs.
6. Add dates, orange juice, and spices, and mix until you get a crumbly crust texture.
7. Press 2/3 of crust into a parchment-lined 8-inch square baking dish, and spread the fig puree evenly over the crust.
8. Take the remainder of the crust mixture and crumble evenly over the filling.
9. Refrigerate for 20-30 minutes. Then cut into bars or squares. (Store in refrigerator or freezer)

**(Fig Bars pictured with dried figs at right→)**

**Dressing/Dip Choices:**

### Creamy Curry Dressing

(One of my favorite recipes by Molly Patrick, from cleanfooddirtygirl.com)

- 3 dates
- 1/4 cup tahini
- 1 tsp curry
- 1 garlic clove
  1 tsp grated ginger
- 1/4 tsp salt
- 1 tbsp lemon juice
- 1/2 cup water

Place all ingredients in a blender and combine until smooth and creamy. (Store extra dressing in the refrigerator for up to seven days.)

### Creamy Curry Dressing Drizzle on a Green Wrap

Dressings are not just for salads. They add flavor to many dishes!

### Strawberry Hemp Dressing

(One of my favorite recipes by Molly Patrick, from cleanfooddirtygirl.com)

- 2 tbsp lemon juice
- 1 tbsp apple cider vinegar
- 3 tbsp coconut aminos (or Bragg's Liquid Aminos)
- 2 tbsp water
- 12 strawberries
- 3 tbsp hemp seeds
- 1/4 tsp garlic powder or granules (or 1 clove garlic)
- 1/4 tsp salt
- Pinch of black pepper

Place all ingredients in a blender and combine until smooth and creamy. (Store extra dressing in the refrigerator for up to three days.)

### Creamy Mustard Dressing

(One of my favorite recipes by Molly Patrick, from cleanfooddirtygirl.com)

- 1/2 cup sunflower seeds
- 1 tbsp tahini
- 1 clove of garlic
- 2 tsp mustard
- 1 tsp brown rice vinegar
- 1 tbsp coconut aminos (or Bragg's Liquid Aminos)
- 1/2 tsp sea salt
- 3/4 cup water

1. Optional: add sunflower seeds to a skillet heated on low for several minutes, toast four minutes, stir often.
2. Place all ingredients in a blender and combine until smooth and creamy.
3. (Store extra dressing in the refrigerator for up to seven days.)

### Hemp Seed Brazil Nut Power Dressing

(One of my favorite recipes by Ani Phyo in "Ani's Raw Food Kitchen")

- 3/4 cup Brazil nuts
- 2 cloves of garlic
- 1 tbsp grated ginger (use microplane)
- 1 tsp sea salt
- 1/4 cup hemp oil
- 2 tbsp lime juice
- 1/4 cup water

1. Use the back of a spoon to peel the ginger. Then grate it with a microplane.
2. Process nuts, garlic, ginger, and salt. Add oil, lime juice, and water, and process until smooth.
3. (Store extra dressing in the refrigerator for up to four days.)

**Turmeric Tahini Dressing**

- 1/3 cup tahini
- 1/3 cup lemon juice
- 1/4 cup plain non-dairy yogurt
- 2 tbsp water
- 1 tbsp olive oil
- 3/4 tsp turmeric
- 1 clove of garlic
- 1/2 tsp sea salt
- 1/4 tsp black pepper

Place all ingredients in a blender combine until smooth and creamy. (Store extra dressing in the refrigerator for up to seven days.)

## Basil Parsley Dressing

- 1/4 cup fresh basil leaves
- 1/4 cup fresh parsley
- 2 tbsp olive oil or hemp oil
- 1 tbsp balsamic vinegar
- 2 cloves of garlic
- 1 tsp spicy mustard
- 1 tbsp tamari or Bragg's Liquid Aminos
- 1 tbsp agave or honey

Place all ingredients in a blender and combine until smooth and creamy. (Store extra dressing in the refrigerator for up to three days.)

## Mango Red Pepper Dressing (on this page)

(One of my favorite recipes adapted from Kristina Carrillo-Bucaram fullyraw.com with Dena's Food Prep Tips)

- 1/2 red bell pepper
- 1 1/2 cup chopped, fresh or frozen mango
- 3/4—1-inch piece of fresh ginger
- 2 tbsp tahini
- 2 tbsp lime juice

1. Follow instructions at the end of *Step Seven (Guidelines for Matching Food Prep with the Weekly Meal Plan), Common Food Prep Technique Tips: How to slice and remove the pit from a mango.*
2. Use the back of a spoon to peel the ginger, then grate it with a microplane.
3. Place all ingredients in a blender and combine until smooth and creamy.
4. (Store extra dressing in the refrigerator for up to seven days.)

## Avocado Mango Pistachio Dressing (next page)

(One of my favorite recipes adapted from Kristina Carrillo-Bucaram, fullyraw.com with Dena's Food Prep Tips)

- 1-2 chopped, fresh mangoes
- 1/2 avocado
- 1 cup of orange juice
- 1/4 cup of pistachios
- Handful of fresh cilantro
- 1 green onion, chopped
- 1 tbsp lime juice

Place all ingredients in a blender and combine until smooth and creamy. (Store extra dressing in the refrigerator for up to three days.)

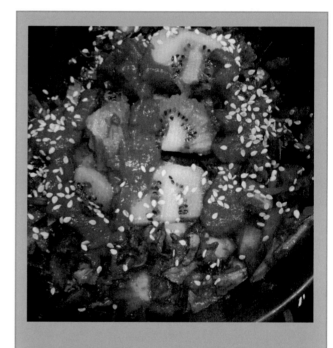

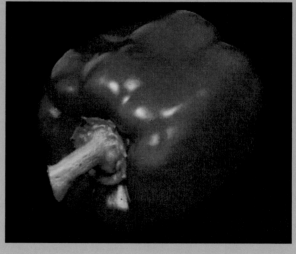

### Mango Date Rosemary Dressing

**(One of my favorite recipes adapted from Kristina Carrillo-Bucaram fullyraw.com with Dena's Food Prep Tips)**

- **3-4 cups chopped, fresh mango**
- **1 cup chopped medjool dates**
- **1 tbsp fresh rosemary**

1. Follow instructions at the end of *Step Seven, Common Food Prep Technique Tips: How to slice and remove the pit from a mango.*

2. Place all ingredients in a blender, add water if needed, combine until smooth and creamy.

3. (Store extra dressing in the refrigerator for up to three days.)

### Tahini Green Dressing

**(One of my favorite recipes adapted from Gena, thehelpinghand.com with Dena's Twist and Food Prep Tips)**

- **1/3 cup tahini**
- **3/4 cup of water**
- **1 clove of garlic, chopped**
- **3 tbsp lime juice**
- **3/4 -1 tsp sea salt**
- **1 cup spinach**
- **1/4 cup of fresh cilantro (can also use parsley)**
- **1 sprig of rosemary**
- **Pinch of black pepper**

Place all ingredients in a blender in the order listed. Then combine until smooth and creamy. (Store extra dressing in the refrigerator for up to three days.)

### Liquid Gold Dressing

**(One of my favorite recipes by Brenda Davis, R.D., & Vesanto Melina M.S., R.D., in "Becoming Vegan")**

- **1/2 cup flaxseed oil**
- **1/2 cup water**
- **1/2 cup lemon juice**
- **2 tbsp balsamic vinegar**
- **1/4 cup Bragg's Liquid Aminos or tamari**
- **1/4 to 1/2 cup nutritional yeast**
- **2 tsp mustard**
- **1 tsp cumin**

Combine all ingredients in the blender. Store in a Mason jar with a lid in the refrigerator for up to 2 weeks. (2 tbsp provide 40-80% of your B12 daily requirement, depending on the amount of nutritional yeast you add.)

### Cashew Chlorella Dill Dressing

- **1/2 cup cashews (soaked 15-30 minutes)**
- **1 medjool date (pre-soaked for 10 minutes)**
- **1 1/2 tbsp. lemon juice**
- **1 1/2 cloves of garlic chopped**
- **3/4 tsp sea salt**
- **1 1/2 tsp dried dill**
- **1 tsp onion powder**
- **3/4 cup of water**
- **1/2 tsp chlorella**

Place all ingredients in a blender. Combine until smooth and creamy. (Store extra dressing in the refrigerator for up to seven days.)

## Apple Curry Dressing

**(Based on a great recipe adapted from Ani Phyo in "Ani's Raw Food Kitchen" with Dena's Food Prep Tips)**

- **1/2 cup each of olive oil and hemp oil (total 1 cup)**
- **2 tbsp lemon juice**
- **1 large, tart apple (skin on), chopped in bite-sized pieces**
- **1 tbsp curry powder**
- **1 tbsp fresh ginger, grated (use microplane)**
- **1 clove of garlic, peeled and chopped**
- **1/2 tsp sea salt**

1. Use the back of a spoon to peel the ginger, then grate with a microplane (totaling 1 tbsp).
2. Place all ingredients in a blender in the order listed and combine until smooth and creamy.
3. (Store extra dressing in the refrigerator for up to three days.)

## Orange Sesame Dressing

**(Based on a great recipe adapted from "Vegetarian Times", July/August 2015, featured here with Dena's Food Prep Tips)**

- **2 tsp fresh ginger, grated (use microplane)**
- **2 tsp orange zest, grated (use microplane)**
- **1/2 cup orange juice**
- **3 tbsp olive oil or flaxseed oil**
- **2 tbsp apple cider vinegar**
- **1 tbsp sesame oil**
- **1 tbsp lime juice**
- **1 tsp Bragg's Liquid Aminos or tamari**
- **2 tbsp tahini**
- **2 tbsp coconut sugar**
- **3/4 tsp sea salt**

1. Use the back of a spoon to peel the ginger. Then grate it with a microplane.
2. Zest orange with microplane. Then juice it (totaling 1/2 cup).
3. Place all ingredients in a blender in the order listed, and combine until smooth and creamy.

4. (Store extra dressing in the refrigerator for up to seven days.)

## Asian Dressing

**(One of my favorite recipes by Nomi Shannon in "The Raw Gourmet")**

- 1 tbsp fresh ginger, grated (use microplane)
- 3-4 tbsp of water
- 4 tbsp of Bragg's Liquid Aminos or tamari
- 1 tbsp sesame oil
- 1 tbsp flaxseed oil
- 2 tbsp tahini
- 1/4 cup scallions, chopped
- 1 tbsp honey
- 1 clove of garlic, peeled and chopped
- 1/4 tsp Chinese 5-spice powder
- 1/4 tsp cumin
- Pinch cayenne

Place all ingredients in a blender in the order listed, and combine until smooth and creamy. (Store extra dressing in the refrigerator for up to seven days.)

## Lentil Cashew Dip

- 1 cup cooked lentils
- 3/4 cup cashews
- 1/2 cup of water
- 2 tbsp lemon juice
- 1 tbsp nutritional yeast
- 1/2-1 clove of garlic, chopped
- 2 tbsp hemp or olive oil
- 3/4 tsp sea salt

**Variation: Lentil Cumin Rosemary Dip**

- Substitute lime juice for lemon juice.
- Add 1/2 cup fresh cilantro, chopped
- Add 1 tsp each cumin and rosemary

Place all ingredients in a food processor and combine until smooth. (Store extra dip in the refrigerator for up to three days.)

## Pea and Edamame Guacamole Dip

- 1 1/2 cup frozen peas (unthawed)
- 1/2 cup frozen organic edamame (unthawed)
- 1 avocado, chopped in quarters
- 4 green onions, white and green parts chopped
- 3 cloves of garlic, chopped
- 1/3 cup fresh cilantro, tightly packed
- 5 tbsp lime juice
- 1/4-1/2 tsp sea salt

1. Place peas and edamame in a bowl of hot water for five minutes to unthaw, and drain prior to processing.
2. Place all ingredients in a food processor, and combine until smooth (add water if needed).
3. (Store extra dip in the refrigerator for up to two days.)

## Black Bean Cilantro Dip

- 1 cup black beans, rinsed
- 2 tbsp lime juice
- 1-2 tbsp olive oil
- 1/4 cup of cashews
- 1/4 cup of fresh cilantro
- 2 cloves of garlic, chopped
- 1/4 cup red pepper, chopped
- 3/4 tsp sea salt

Add all ingredients into the food processor. Add water to achieve desired consistency. Can be used as a salad dressing with a thinner consistency. (Store extra dip in the refrigerator for up to three days.)

## Pinto Bean Basil Dip

- 1 cup pinto beans, rinsed
- 2 tbsp lemon juice
- 1-2 tbsp hemp oil
- 1/4 cup of Brazil nuts
- 1/4 cup of fresh basil
- 2 cloves of garlic, chopped
- 1 tbsp nutritional yeast
- 3/4 tsp sea salt

Add all ingredients into the food processor. Add water to achieve desired consistency. Can be used as a salad dressing with a thinner consistency. (Store extra dip in the refrigerator for up to three days.)

## Hummus—Traditional and Variations

Hummus is a Middle Eastern dip made of garbanzo beans (chickpeas) mashed with oil, garlic, lemon juice, and tahini. **Several variations of hummus are shown at far right:**

- **Traditional hummus topped with pumpkin seeds and paprika (with seaweed sheets for dipping),**
- **Cilantro hummus, and**
- **Bean-free sun-dried tomato hummus.**

## Traditional Hummus

- 15 oz can of garbanzo beans, rinsed
- 1/8-1/4 cup tahini
- 2 tbsp lemon juice
- 2 tbsp olive oil
- 1-2 cloves of garlic, chopped
- 1 tsp cumin
- 3/4 tsp sea salt
- Pinch of black pepper

Place all in processor and combine until smooth. If too thick, add water slowly.

## Cilantro Hummus

Same as Traditional Hummus. Just add 1/2 cup tightly-packed fresh cilantro, chopped.

## Sumac Hummus

- 2 cups garbanzo beans, rinsed and drained
- Start with a 1/4 cup water (add up to 1/2 cup water, depending on consistency)
- 2 tbsp olive oil
- 1/8 cup tahini
- 1 tsp sumac
- 1 tsp sea salt
- 2 tbsp lime juice
- 2 cloves of garlic, chopped

Process all ingredients until smooth.

## Sun-dried Tomato Hummus (Bean-free)

(One of my favorite recipes by Ani Phyo in "Ani's Raw Food Kitchen")

- 2 cups zucchini, chopped
- 2 cloves of garlic, chopped
- 2 tbsp lemon juice
- 1/4 cup plus 1 tbsp olive oil
- 1/2 cup tahini
- 1 tsp sea salt
- 2 tbsp fresh parsley, chopped
- 1/3 cup sun-dried tomatoes, chopped
- Pinch of paprika

1. Place all ingredients through salt in processor, and process until smooth.
2. Place mixture in a bowl and stir in parsley and sun-dried tomatoes.
3. Set aside for 10 minutes, then enjoy.
4. (Store extra hummus in the refrigerator for two days.)

**Cauliflower Hummus**

(One of my favorite recipes by Isa Chandra Moskowitz & Terry Hope Romero in "Veganomicon")

- **Small head of cauliflower, chopped**
- **2-3 cloves of garlic, chopped**
- **1 1/2 cups of garbanzo beans, rinsed**
- **2 tbsp tahini**
- **1 tbsp olive oil**
- **1/4 cup scallions, chopped**
- **1/4 cup fresh parsley**
- **1/2 tsp sea salt**
- **2 tsp cumin**
- **1/4 tsp paprika**
- **2 tbsp lemon juice**

1. Boil cauliflower for 12-15 minutes, cool slightly, and puree a bit in processor.
2. Add remaining ingredients, and process until smooth. Add water if needed for desired consistency.
3. (Store extra hummus in the refrigerator for two days.)

## Broccoli Pea Blend

**(Based on a great recipe adapted from Ani Phyo in "Ani's Raw Food Kitchen" featured here with Dena's Twist and Food Prep Tips)**

- **1 clove of garlic, chopped**
- **Pinch of black pepper**
- **1 tsp sea salt**
- **1 cup Brazil nuts**
- **1 1/2 cups of broccoli, chopped**
- **1 cup peas, frozen**

1. Place peas in a bowl of hot water for five minutes to unthaw, and drain prior to processing.
2. Process the garlic, pepper, and salt into small pieces.
3. Add Brazil nuts, and process into a powder
4. Remove from processor and set aside in a bowl.
5. Process broccoli and peas while slowly adding the garlic nut powder back in.

## Citrus Date Sesame Sauce

**(One of my favorite recipes by Isa Chandra Moskowitz & Terry Hope Romero in "Veganomicon")**

- **1 1/4 cups orange juice**
- **1/2 cup medjool dates, chopped**
- **1/2 cup tahini**
- **2 tbsp sesame seeds**
- **2 tbsp miso**
- **1/4 tsp cardamom**
- **Sea salt and pepper**

1. Soak the dates in the orange juice for 2 hours, then process until creamy.
2. Add the remaining ingredients and blend.
3. Season with salt/pepper as needed. Great over steamed vegetables, like asparagus!

## Macadamia & Sun-Dried Tomato Spread

- **1 cup raw macadamia nuts**
- **2 tbsp lemon juice**
- **1/2 cup no oil sun-dried tomatoes, chopped**
- **1/4 tsp sea salt**
- **2 tbsp parsley, finely chopped**

1. Process nuts and lemon juice.
2. Add tomatoes and salt, process, and transfer to a bowl. (Mixture will be crumbly.)
3. Mix in parsley, and sprinkle with pepper.

## Traditional Pesto

**Pesto is an Italian-origin sauce of crushed basil leaves, garlic, and oil (no cheese in the plant-based version).**

## Cilantro Pesto with Olives

- **1/3 cup fresh cilantro, chopped**
- **1/4 cup olive oil**
- **2 tbsp fresh parsley, chopped**
- **3 tbsp lemon juice**
- **1/2 tsp cumin**
- **1/4 tsp sea salt**
- **1/4 tsp ground red pepper**
- **2 garlic cloves, chopped**
- **8-10 olives (Kalamata, my favorite) pitted and chopped**

Combine all ingredients except olives and process until smooth. Place in a bowl and fold in olives.

## Parsley Basil Pesto

- **1 cup parsley, tightly packed, chopped**
- **1 cup basil, tightly packed, chopped**
- **1/2 cup green onion, chopped**
- **1/2 cup olive oil**

Combine all ingredients into a food processor and continue to mix until smooth.

**Pistachio Pesto**

(One of my favorite recipes by Christie Bailey in *Raw Food Healing Bible*)

- 2 cloves of garlic, chopped
- 1/2 cup pistachios, chopped
- 1 1/4 cups fresh basil, chopped
- 1 tbsp lemon juice
- 1/2 tsp sea salt
- 1 tbsp nutritional yeast flakes
- 5 tbsp olive oil, flax or hemp oil
- Pinch of black pepper

Process all ingredients until smooth. (Store extra pesto in the refrigerator for up to a week.)

**Soup Choices:**

**Grape Almond Soup**

- 1/2 cup slivered almonds
- 2 1/2 cups green or red grapes
- 1/4 cup green or red grapes, cut in half for garnish
- 3/4 cup almond or hemp milk
- 1 tbsp lime juice
- 2-3 scallions, chopped (cut extra onions for garnish)
- Salt and pepper, to taste

1. Blend almonds in Vitamix dry container, or in food processor, to a powder.
2. Then place in Vitamix liquid container with remaining ingredients. (Reserve 1/4 cup white or red grapes and extra scallions for garnish to be sprinkled on individual soup servings.)
3. Mix until creamy. Serve at room temperature

**Pea Dill Soup with Seed Topping (page 65, left)**

(One of my favorite recipes adapted from Cherie Soria, Brenda Davis, R.D., & Vesanto Melina M.S., R.D., in "The Raw Food Revolution Diet" with Dena's Food Prep Tips)

- 1 cup frozen peas, unthawed
- 1/4 -1/2 cup water
- 1/4 -1/2 small orange, chopped
- 2 tsp miso
- 1/2 tsp onion powder
- 1/2 tsp garlic powder
- salt and pepper to taste
- 2 tsp dried dill
- Sunflower, pumpkin or hemp seeds for garnish

1. Place peas in a bowl of hot water for five minutes to unthaw. Drain prior to processing.
2. Place all ingredients in the order listed in a Vitamix. (Start with 1/4 cup water and add more as needed to blend and achieve desired thickness.)

3. Add dill and blend gently.
4. Pour soup in bowls and sprinkle with seed of choice.

## Cauliflower Quinoa Hummus Soup (65, top)

**(Based on a great recipe adapted from Alyssa Rimmer from www.simplyquinoa.com featured here with Dena's Food Prep Tips)**

**An ideal soup to make when you have leftover hummus and quinoa!**

- **Soak 1/2 cup cashews for 1 hour**
- **Small head of cauliflower, chopped into small florets**
- **Small sweet potato, chopped in bite-sized cubes**
- **One head of garlic**
- **1/2 cup hummus (see *Traditional Hummus Recipe, Dips Recipe Section*)**
- **1/2 cup quinoa, cooked**
- **2 cups vegetable broth**
- **2 cups water**
- **3 tsp nutritional yeast**
- **2 tsp miso**
- **Salt and pepper**

1. Preheat oven to 425°
2. Soak cashews for 1 hour. During this time, if not using leftover hummus or quinoa, prepare these ingredients.
   a. For hummus, see *Traditional Hummus Recipe, Dips Recipe Section*.
   b. For quinoa, bring 1 cup of water to a boil, add 1/2 cup quinoa, and simmer for 15 minutes or until water is absorbed. This will give you extra quinoa to incorporate into other meals.
3. Place chopped cauliflower and sweet potato into a large bowl and toss with a small amount of avocado or coconut oil and salt and pepper.
4. Transfer mixture evenly into a rectangular casserole dish lined with parchment paper.
5. Take the entire garlic head and chop off the top to expose the cloves. Drizzle with a small

amount of oil and salt and pepper. Prepare for roasting by wrapping in foil.
6. Place the cauliflower/potato mixture and garlic head in the oven together and roast for 25-30 minutes.
7. Add vegetable broth to Vitamix plus half of the roasted vegetables, and squeeze out the roasted garlic cloves from the head of garlic. (Reserve a few cloves to use as a topping on the soup). Blend slowly until well mixed.
8. Add water, remaining vegetable mixture, drained cashews, quinoa, and hummus, blending until creamy.
9. Add miso, nutritional yeast, salt, and pepper, and blend until well mixed.
10. Pour soup into bowls, and add optional toppings: a drizzle of olive oil or avocado oil, the reserved roasted garlic, some chopped parsley or cilantro, chopped scallions, and/or pumpkin seeds.

## Carrot Curry Soup with Macadamia Nuts (65→)

**(Based on a great recipe adapted from "Vegetarian Times", October 2012, with Dena's Food Prep Tips)**

- **1 1/4 pounds carrots, grated**
- **2 cups leeks or scallions, thinly sliced**
- **2 tbsp olive oil**
- **1/4 heaping tsp baking soda**
- **1 tsp curry powder (add more if you like it spicy)**
- **4 cups of water or vegetable stock**
- **1/4 cup macadamia nuts, chopped (you can also use pistachios or your favorite seeds, like hemp)**

1. Grate carrots, slice scallions, and set aside.
2. Place olive oil in a large pot, heat to medium, and add carrots, scallions, and baking soda. Cook covered for 12-15 minutes. Control the heat and stir occasionally so only a small amount of browning occurs.
3. Stir in curry, and mix for about 20 seconds. Add water and simmer for 10 minutes. Taste and add salt as needed.

4. In small batches, transfer mixture to a Vitamix (use caution transferring the hot mixture), and continue until all ingredients are well blended, or use an immersion blender directly in the pot.

5. Pour into soup bowls and top with chopped nuts or seeds of choice.

**Honeydew and Cucumber Soup (not shown)**

**(One of my favorite recipes adapted from Eco Chef Bryan Au in "Raw Star Recipes Cookbook" with Dena's Food Prep Tips)**

- **3 cups of water**
- **1 small honeydew melon, chopped**
- **1 cucumber, chopped**
- **1 tbsp fresh mint, chopped**

1. Remove the melon rind and chop the melon. (Follow instructions, *How to remove the rind and slice a melon:* as described in *Common Food Prep Technique Tips, Step Seven*)

2. Blend all ingredients (through cucumber) in a Vitamix until smooth. Add mint and blend gently.

3. Pour into bowls and garnish with extra mint and small pieces of cucumber.

## Meal Choices

Dishes in this category are separated into "Light Meals/Veggie Side Dishes" that can be combined to make full meals, "Salad Stand-outs," and "Legumes/Soy/Fermented Soy/Grains." These recipes can be interchanged for lunch or dinner depending on your appetite and when you choose to eat your larger meal for the day.

## Light Meals/Veggie Side Dishes

All of the following recipes can easily be modified to incorporate your favorite vegetables, dressings, fillings, and toppings. That means in this section alone you could create over thirty light meals/veggie side dishes that accommodate your unique taste buds using the recipes I have provided as guidelines. **For example, see the Romaine Wrap with Fig Pistachio Filling shown at the bottom right of page 65.**

## Vegetables as a Side Dish or Light Meal

Vegetables can be eaten raw, boiled, steamed, roasted, or fried. Regardless of cooking method, vegetables should not be overcooked (until they're watery or soggy, or they lose their shape from their raw form). Rather, they should still maintain some crispness and/or browning if roasted. Retention of nutrients can be altered based generally on the cooking method. The worst method for preserving nutrients is frying, and I don't ever recommend this method for vegetable (or any food product) preparation. With that said, there are always trade-offs for using different cooking methods. It is true that cooking can degrade some nutrients, but it can also enhance the availability of others. Let's take a look at nutrient categories and how cooking vegetables changes their nutrient profile.

**Water-soluble nutrients (e.g., Vitamins B and C, anti-oxidant polyphenols)** are the most vulnerable to degradation of nutrients in cooking and processing (canning, freezing). Cooking fresh spinach removes about two-thirds of its Vitamin C. However, frozen spinach can have higher levels of Vitamin C then fresh spinach (counter to the processing nutrient degradation rule). This is dependent on the time from harvest of fresh spinach to the amount of time spent in storage and transport, to availability to you, the consumer.

**Fat-soluble nutrients (Vitamins A, D, E, and K and anti-oxidant carotenoids)** are better preserved during cooking and processing.

To complicate matters further, no one cooking method (boiled, steamed, roasted) is superior over another or over raw consumption of vegetables because each method may enhance the availability of one nutrient in a specific vegetable while degrading another nutrient. For example, boiling carrots increases carotenoids as compared to eating raw carrots, but boiling destroys polyphenols in carrots, so if you want to increase this nutrient, eat your carrots raw! The bottom line is to keep rotating, not only the vegetables you eat, but the manner in which you prepare them.

## Roasted Veggies (baked in the oven using dry heat, resulting in a crispy texture)

**Great veggies for roasting include: beets, cauliflower, sweet potatoes, yams, Brussel sprouts, broccoli (see Tahini Roasted Broccoli, below). The smaller the size of the chopped vegetables, the faster they will roast.**

1. Place chopped veggies in a bowl, add herbs/spices, garlic/onions (if using), small amount of oil (see charts to ensure using oils with high smoke point) or dressing, mix, and place in a baking dish lined with parchment paper.

2. Roast in the oven at 400°-450° for 10 minutes to 50 minutes (broccoli versus yams), depending on the density of the vegetable.

3. Roasted vegetables can be a side dish all on their own or combine with a protein during roasting (e.g., beans, tempeh) for a light meal.

## Roasted Broccoli with Tahini

1. Chop up 4-5 cups of broccoli florets and thin stems, and place in a large bowl.

2. Mix up the tahini dressing:

- **2 tbsp tahini**
- **1 tbsp avocado oil**
- **1 tbsp lemon juice**
- **1 tbsp coconut aminos**
- **2 tsp nutritional yeast**
- **1-2 cloves of garlic chopped or minced**

3. Add to broccoli, mix, and spread evenly, either on a parchment-lined baking sheet, or a casserole dish. Roast at 450° for 10 minutes.

## Roasted Cauliflower with Tahini and Garlic

1. Use the dressing from *Roasted Broccoli with Tahini.*

2. Prepare in the same manner, but add chopped red onion and whole garlic cloves to the mixture before placing in a casserole dish.

3. Roast at 400° for 45-50 minutes. Half way through roasting period, remove from oven, mix to prevent over browning, return to oven, and finish roasting.

4. The last 10 minutes of roasting, add 1 cup of chopped mushrooms, mix with the cauliflower, and finish the roasting time.

## Roasted Beets with Orange and Dill

1. Preheat oven to 400°.

2. Peel beets, trim both ends, and chop into bite-sized pieces. (Wear gloves or wash hands immediately after handling beets to reduce red hand staining.)

3. Place in a bowl and toss in 1-2 tsp olive oil and 1/4-1/2 cup of orange juice.

4. Sprinkle with 1 tbsp dried dill and 1/2 tsp salt.

5. Place in a parchment-lined roasting pan large enough to spread the beets out as evenly as possible and bake for 50 minutes – one hour.

6. Half way through roasting period, remove from oven, mix to prevent over browning, return to oven, and finish roasting.

## Steamed Veggies

**A steamer basket is placed over a pot of boiling water and covered with a lid so veggies have no contact with water and are rapidly cooked.**

The smaller the size of the chopped vegetables, the faster they will steam. Different from roasting, vegetables should be steamed first, then transferred to a large bowl and sprinkled with herbs and oil/dressing (if using). Steam time can range from 3-20 minutes depending on the density of the vegetable. Steamed vegetables can be a side dish all on their own or combine with a protein after steaming (e.g., beans, tempeh) for a light meal.

## Asparagus and Snow Peas

1. Wash both vegetables, snap off both ends of each snow pea, and pull off the side strings (found along the pea length-wise top and bottom). Chop into bite sized pieces.

2. Place both veggies in a steamer basket for 5 minutes. Then remove immediately.

3. Place into a bowl and toss with a light dressing of your choice from our dressing recipes.

## Boiled Veggies

**Boil a small amount of water in a pot and add vegetables. When completed, reserve boiling water for soup base or dips to take advantage of nutrient-filled water.**

The longer and more submerged vegetables are under water, the greater amount of heat-sensitive, water-souble nutrient loss into the water. Conversely, antioxidants in tomatoes and carrots are three to four times more available during consumption when cooked. In these instances, heating releases the antioxidants that are trapped in the fibrous part of the vegetable.

Boiling time can range from 3-20 minutes depending on the density of the vegetable. Boiled vegetables can be a side dish all on their own or combine with a protein after boiling (e.g., beans, tempeh) for a light meal.

### Raw Veggies (Not Including Greens)

The reason people get tired of eating vegetables in general is that they always eat the same vegetables prepared the same way. In addition to practicing diversity in vegetable consumption, rotating through the different cooking techniques listed above can defeat the hum-drum of food boredom. The same is true when consuming raw vegetables.

Since you don't have the opportunity to "mix it up" with cooking methods, you must rely on different textures. There are numerous ways to chop, slice, and grate every vegetable, which can actually change the taste and influence the manner in which you integrate it into a recipe and attain the overall goal of increased consumption! Raw vegetables can be prepared in their natural whole food state (washed and peeled); as a liquid in the form of a juice or smoothie, dressing, dip; or blended into a raw soup.

A few examples of different ways to eat raw vegetables include:

- Just munch (e.g., carrots, celery, snow peas) or Crudité dipped into any of the dips listed in the Dressings/Dips section
- Smoothies (*Dena's Basic Green Smoothie and Variations*)
- Dressings (*Mango Red Pepper Dressing*)
- Dips (*Green Pea Guacamole Dip, Broccoli Pea Blend, and Macadamia & Sun-dried Tomato Spread*)
- Soups (*Pea Dill with Sunflower Seeds Soup and Honeydew and Cucumber Soup*)
- Filling for Green Wraps
- Zoodles (or cucumber, carrot, or beet raw noodles)

**Pictured at left:**
- **Roasted Brussels sprouts**
- **Steamed eggplant zucchini medley**
- **Raw vegetable assortment**

### Wraps

Wraps come in different healthy forms including swiss chard, romaine, collard greens, and store-bought vegan wraps like spinach and coconut wraps. Be creative with filling combinations (raw vegetables, greens, grains, legumes, fermented soy, fruits, nuts, seeds, seaweed granules) and dressings/dips. Roll those babies up and eat or slice into bite-sized pieces. Remember, if you are using the wrap as a Light Meal, include a protein source in the filling in whole food form (e.g., beans, quinoa) or as part of the dressing/dip (e.g., *Lentil Cashew Dip*). If the wrap is a side dish, make sure to combine it with a second side dish protein source to round out your meal.

coconut WRAP MANIA

### Zoodles

**Zucchini Noodles made by spiralizing, slicing, or julienne-peeling zucchini into noodle/pasta form. Can also be done with carrots, beets, cucumbers, and cabbage for a low fat and calorie pasta exchange.**

Zoodle is a term combining zucchini and noodle into one word. The calorie comparison of 1 cup of pasta at 221 calories and 43g carbohydrates to 1 cup of zoodles at 25 calories and 4.6g carbohydrates may encourage you to try this unique plant-based specialty.

My favorite method for creating zoodles is to use an inexpensive spiralizer. Use organic zucchini so you can spiralize and eat the entire vegetable without peeling.

1. Wash the zucchini, and chop off both ends of the zucchini to create a flat surface.

2. Place the wider end into the plastic spiked handle side and the narrow end up against the blade to secure the zucchini in place.

3. Now twist the handle, push the veggie forward into the blade, and collect the zoodles in a bowl on the opposite side of the blade.

The spiralizer comes with 2-3 different blades to change the thickness and shape of zoodles and/or to make veggie chips. I personally like to eat my zoodles raw, at room temperature, with a delicious sauce and other chopped veggies like mushrooms, tomatoes, and tempeh, plus I mix in some greens. You can also lightly stir-fry the zoodles, which softens and warms them.

### Sesame Oil Cucumber and Miso Mix

**(A great recipe adapted from "Cooking Light Magazine", May 2011, with Dena's Food Prep Tips)**

- **1 1/2 tbsp toasted sesame seeds**
- **2 tbsp miso**
- **1 tbsp honey**
- **1 tbsp rice vinegar**
- **1 tbsp water, heated**
- **2 tsp sesame oil**

FIG ZOODLE SALAD

- **1 tsp crushed red pepper**
- **4 cups cucumber, sliced thinly (can use the slicing attachment on the food processor)**

**Toasting sesame seeds, 2 methods** (will keep for months if stored in an air-tight container in the refrigerator.):

- **Method One, Stove Top:** Use a medium fry pan. Spread 1/2 cup sesame seeds evenly in pan and cook on medium/medium-low heat for 4-5 minutes. The seeds will burn quickly, so throughout the cooking time, either shake the pan or stir the seeds with a wooden spoon until they become a light golden-brown color. Allow to cool, and then add to recipes.

- **Method Two, Oven Toasting:** Preheat oven to 350° and line a cooking sheet with parchment paper. Pour sesame seeds onto the cooking sheet in an even layer and place in the oven. Shake the tray and check for a light golden-brown color in 5-minute increments. Allow to cool, and then add to recipe.

Combine all ingredients except cucumber in a large bowl and mix using a whisk until well combined. Add cucumber and toss in the dressing carefully, so as not to damage the cucumbers with a large spoon. Eat immediately, or store in the refrigerator.

### Salad Standouts

Greens are an integral part of your new healthy plant-based lifestyle. Often people ask me if I get tired of eating salads. I never do. Actually, my body craves these nutrient-rich greens, and I have a huge arsenal of dressing recipes that I rotate. I also vary the type and combination of greens, the salad boosters (proteins, other vegetables, and fruits), and the toppings (nuts, seeds, dried fruits, and sea vegetables). This approach makes it easy to select different flavors and textures and create tons of options.

It's important to categorize your greens as "tough" or "delicate." This will be helpful when you choose a dressing. Pair thicker dressings with the tough greens that taste better after having the opportunity to marinate in these dressings. Drizzle lighter dressings over delicate greens. Otherwise they will wilt, become soggy quickly, and mask the unique flavors of the greens. Nothing's worse than an overdressed salad!

- **Tough Greens:** Kale, romaine, spinach, cabbage (green, purple), and collard greens
- **Delicate Greens:** Watercress, red or green leaf lettuce, butter lettuce (Bibb and Boston), arugula (peppery flavor, but less nutrients than other greens), swiss chard, and beet greens

With that said, I am sharing some of my favorite "Salad Standouts." Not all of these recipes include greens. As I keep saying, there are many healthy options within each of these food categories for you to enjoy. As you become more comfortable in the plant-based lifestyle, start creating your own Green Masterpieces!

### Papaya Avocado with Mixed Greens

- **1 medium-sized ripe papaya**
- **1 medium-sized ripe avocado**
- **2 tbsp scallions, sliced**
- **2 cups greens (mix it up with kale, mustard greens, and spinach)**
- **Pistachios or macadamia nuts, optional**

Dressing:

- **1/3 cup rice vinegar**
- **1/4 cup hemp oil or flaxseed oil**
- **3 tbsp papaya seeds**
- **3 tbsp white onion, chopped**
- **2 tbsp coconut sugar**
- **1/4 tsp salt**
- **1/4 tsp dry mustard powder**

### Prep Work One: Peel and Chop

1. Peel the papaya (follow instructions, *How to remove the skin and slice a papaya:* as described in *Common Food Prep Technique Tips, Step Seven*).

2. Place the seeds from the interior of the papaya into the Vitamix, and place bite-sized cubes of the fruit in a large salad bowl.

3. Cut the avocado in bite-sized pieces (follow instructions, *How to open an avocado and cut bite-sized pieces of flesh:* as described in *Common Food Prep Technique Tips, Step Seven*). Place pieces in the salad bowl with papaya.

4. Slice the scallions and place in the salad bowl.

5. Chop the white onion and place in the Vitamix with the papaya seeds.

### Prep Work Two: Make the Dressing

Add rice vinegar, hemp oil, coconut sugar, salt, and mustard powder to Vitamix that already contains papaya seeds and white onion. Blend until papaya seeds look like small black specs.

### Prep Work Three: Combine Salad

1. Add mixed greens to salad bowl that contains papaya, avocado, and scallions.

2. Pour the dressing from the Vitamix over the mixture and gently mix so as not to break up the papaya and avocado squares. Top with pistachios or macadamia nuts, if desired.

### Blueberry Beet and Walnut Salad

- **3-4 medium red beets, roasted**
- **1/3 cup lime juice**
- **2 tbsp hemp oil**
- **2 tbsp honey**
- **2 tsp spicy mustard**
- **1 tbsp ginger, grated with microplane**
- **1/8-1/4 tsp Himalayan sea salt and pepper**
- **4 cups organic blueberries**
- **1/2 cup walnuts, toasted**
- **1/2 cup pecans, toasted**
- **1/2 cup mint or dill, chopped**

### Prep Work One: Preheat Oven to 350°

Place walnuts and pecans (not chopped) on a rimmed baking sheet and bake 5-10 minutes. Check frequently and mix as needed to prevent burning. Set aside and then chop, totaling 1 cup of nuts.

**Prep Work Two: Turn Oven up to 400°**

1. Peel beets, trim both ends, and chop into bite-sized pieces. Wear gloves or wash hands immediately after handling beets to reduce red hand staining.

2. Place in a bowl and toss in 1-2 tsp olive oil.

3. Place in a parchment-lined roasting pan large enough to spread the beets out as evenly as possible and bake for 50 minutes to one hour. Half way through roasting period, remove from oven and mix to prevent over browning. Then return to oven and finish roasting.

4. After roasting, allow to cool prior to adding to other salad ingredients.

**Prep Work Three:**

Peel a knob of ginger using the back of a spoon and grate using a microplane for 1 tbsp ginger.

**Prep Work Four: Make Dressing**

Combine ingredients from lime juice through salt and pepper in a small bowl and mix thoroughly with a whisk. In a large salad bowl, add cooled beets, blueberries, nuts, and mint/dill and toss with dressing.

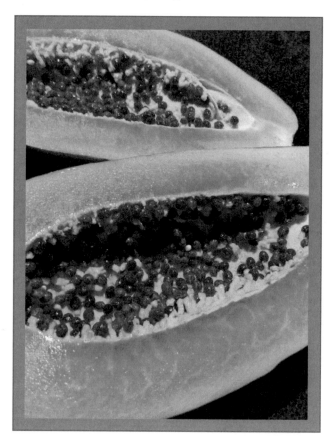

**Cabbage Carrot Cucumber Slaw with Ginger Orange Tahini**

(A favorite recipe adapted from "Vegetarian Times", July/August 2015, with Dena's Food Prep Tips)

**Salad Ingredients:**

- 3 cups green cabbage, chopped fine
- 2 cups red cabbage, chopped fine

- 1 cup green or red pepper, sliced lengthwise
- 1 cup cucumber, peeled and julienned (cut in thin strips like matchsticks)
- 3/4 cup carrots, julienned
- 1 cup sunflower or pumpkin seeds
- 1/2 cup fresh mint, finely chopped

Dressing Ingredients:

- 1 tsp orange zest, use microplane
- 1/2 cup orange juice
- 3 tbsp olive oil
- 2 tbsp apple cider vinegar
- 2 tbsp tahini
- 2 tbsp coconut sugar
- 1 tbsp toasted sesame oil
- 1 tbsp lime juice
- 2 tsp ginger, finely chopped
- 1 tsp tamari (or Bragg's Liquid Aminos or Coconut Aminos)
- 3/4 tsp Himalayan sea salt

**Prep Work One: Chop, Slice, Zest, Juice**

1. Chop/slice green and red cabbage, pepper, cucumber, carrot, and mint, and place in a large salad bowl.
2. Wash one orange. Use a microplane, zest the orange to yield 1 tsp of zest, and place it in the Vitamix.
3. Juice the orange into the Vitamix to yield 1/2 cup of orange juice.
4. Peel a one-inch knob of ginger and chop to yield 2 tsp. Place it in the Vitamix.

**Prep Work Two: Make Dressing**

Add olive oil, apple cider vinegar, tahini, coconut sugar, sesame oil, lime juice, tamari, and salt to the Vitamix that already contains orange zest, orange juice, and ginger. Blend until smooth.

**Prep Work Three: Combine Salad**

Pour dressing from Vitamix over salad ingredients in the salad bowl. Start with a small amount, mix, and add more dressing as needed so greens aren't soaked. Once plated, top with sunflower or pumpkin seeds.

**Apricot Beet Salad with Apples and Cinnamon**

**(Great dish to make in advance and refrigerate)**

- 3/4 cup nuts (walnuts or pecans or combination), toasted
- 1 Fuji apple, peeled and grated with box grater

- 2 red beets (about 1/2 pound), peeled and grated with box grater
- 1/2 cup dried apricots, chopped into bite-sized pieces
- Zest 1 tsp orange zest, then juice 2 tbsp of the orange
- 2 tbsp honey
- 1 tsp cinnamon
- 1/2 tsp ground nutmeg
- 1/8 tsp salt

1. Preheat oven to 350°
2. Leave the nuts whole and spread them on a parchment-lined cookie sheet in a single layer.
3. Bake for 5-10 minutes. Check frequently until nuts become darker in color and you can smell them roasting.
4. When roasting is completed, allow nuts to cool. Then chop nuts.
5. Zest orange first. Then cut orange in half and juice to equal 2 tbsp.
6. Peel the apple, grate it with the box grater, and place it in a large bowl.
7. Peel the beets, grate them, and add to the bowl with the apple. Wash your hands immediately to reduce red beet stains.
8. Place all remaining ingredients into the large bowl and mix until well blended.
9. Place in the refrigerator for at least 30 minutes for best flavor.

## Legumes/Soy/Fermented Soy/Grains

The recipes in this section are complete meals that include a protein source, vegetable, and dressing or sauce. I love these recipes, and I usually prepare them for special dinners or dinner parties. If you don't have time during the week to prepare an elaborate dinner, choose an item from one of these recipes (e.g., choose the protein source and follow cooking methods in the recipe), and use whatever vegetables you have in the refrigerator (which may differ from those specified in the recipe), or add a veggie side dish to round out a full meal. Remember plant-based eating is so versatile and allows you to customize every meal to your particular tastes and favorite whole foods.

## Tofu Scramble

**(traditional recipe with endless variations)**

- 1 package extra firm tofu, drained and pressed
- Onion of choice (red—my favorite, scallions) and/or garlic (chopped or minced)
- Any combination of vegetables (red or green pepper, broccoli, zucchini, snow peas, asparagus, eggplant). I use whatever is in the refrigerator.
- 1-2 tsp oil (coconut, avocado, grapeseed)
- 2-3 cups spinach packed tightly (option: don't add spinach to scramble, but arrange spinach on plates and spoon scramble on top)
- Any combination of herbs/spices (basil—can't go wrong just using basil, oregano, thyme, dill, cumin, coriander, curry) or select a dressing from the recipe list (use a heartier/thicker dressing)
- Optional toppings (nuts, seeds, chopped parsley or cilantro), plus cut fruit (strawberries, melon, apples) on the side

1. Drain and press tofu as described in *Step Seven General Food Prep Tips* and set aside.
2. While the tofu is draining, chop onions/garlic if using and chop up vegetables.

3. Heat oil in a large skillet on medium heat, add onions/garlic, and sauté for 30 seconds (don't burn).

4. Add vegetables and sauté for 5 minutes, mixing frequently. If ingredients start to stick to the pan, add small amounts of water and mix.

5. Take tofu, crumble small handfuls into the skillet, and combine with the other ingredients.

6. Gradually add the spinach in handfuls. It will seem like too much for the skillet, but it will cook down. Mix with each addition until all spinach has been added and mixed.

7. Cover the skillet and steam for 5 minutes.

8. Add spices/herbs or dressing and mix well. Then turn off heat.

9. Spoon tofu scramble onto plates, add any toppings, place cut fruit along the border of the plate and serve. Option: place tofu scramble on a bed of spinach, cooked grain, or zoodles.

**Wheatberry Salad with Raisins**

**(A favorite recipe adapted from "Cooking Light Magazine" April 2010, with Dena's Food Prep Tips)**

- **1/2 tsp salt**
- **3 tbsp pistachios**
- **1/4 cup scallions, thinly sliced**
- **1/2 tsp ginger**
- **2 tbsp olive oil**
- **2 tbsp lemon juice**
- **2 tsp honey**
- **1/2 tsp coriander, ground**
- **1/2 cup raisins (golden are best)**
- **2 tbsp cilantro, chopped**

**Prep Work One: Preheat Oven to 350° (in Preparation for Prep Two) and Cook Wheatberries.**

1. In a medium-sized sauce pan, place wheat berries and salt and add water to a level 2 inches above the grain level.

2. Bring to a boil, then reduce to simmer, and cover for 1 hour.

3. After one hour drain off any excess water. Wheatberries should still be chewy when you check to see if done.

4. Add 1/2 cup raisins to hot wheatberries and combine in saucepan.

**Prep Work Two: While Wheatberries Are Cooking, Roast Pistachios.**

Place pistachios (not chopped) on a rimmed baking sheet and bake 5-10 minutes. Check frequently and mix as needed to prevent burning. Set aside and then chop slightly, totaling 3 tbsp.

1. **Prep Work Three: Make Dressing.**
Slice 1/4 cup scallions and set aside.

2. Peel a knob of ginger using the back of a spoon, and grate using a microplane for 1/2 tsp ginger.

3. In a small bowl, add 1⁄4 tsp salt and ingredients from ginger through coriander. Stir with a whisk.

**Prep Work Four: Combine Grain and Dressing**

1. As soon as wheatberries are cooked and still hot, place in a large ceramic or metal bowl, combine with raisins and dressing, and let stand for 15 minutes for raisins to plump and for mixture to completely cool.

2. Then add sliced scallions, cilantro, and pistachios and mix. Serve right away, or make in advance and refrigerate.(Maintains great flavor even a day later when refrigerated.)

### Farro with Red Pepper and Snow Peas

- 2 cups cooked farro
- 1/2 red pepper, chopped
- 1/2 cup snow peas, diagonally sliced
- 1/4 cup mushrooms, chopped
- 1/3 cup scallions, finely sliced

Dressing:

- 3 tbsp sesame oil
- 1 1/2 tbsp soy sauce
- 1 tsp rice vinegar
- 1 tsp ginger, grated with microplane
- 1-2 cloves of garlic, finely chopped
- 1/8 tsp salt and pepper

1. Rinse farro. Then add 1 cup farro to 3 cups of water in a medium-sized kettle and bring to a boil.

2. Turn down to simmer and cover, cooking for 25-30 minutes until water is absorbed. This should make more than 2 cups cooked farro, so save the extra for a lunch or dinner protein source the following day..

3. While farro is cooking, chop the red pepper, snow peas, mushrooms, and scallions.

4. Mix all but scallions into the kettle of cooking farro for the last 10 minutes of the cooking process. Cover and allow to finish cooking.

5. Make the dressing by combining all ingredients in a small bowl and whisking them together.

6. Once the farro is cooked and allowed to cool, add the dressing and scallions and combine all together.

### Ratatouille with Tofu

**(A favorite recipe adapted from Helene An, featured in "Cooking Light Magazine", May 2008, with Dena's Food Prep Tips)**

- 1 cup carrot, finely chopped
- 1/2 cup yellow onion, finely chopped
- 1/4 cup fresh basil, coarsely chopped
- 2 tsp fresh thyme, chopped
- 4 cloves of garlic, minced
- 2 cups (about 12 oz) of extra firm tofu, drained
- 2 cups eggplant, peeled and diced
- 1 cup zucchini, peeled and diced
- 1 cup ripe tomato, chopped
- 4 tsp pesto (use Parsley Basil or Pistachio Pesto from Dip section)
- 2 (14 oz) cans tomato sauce (no salt or sugar added)
- 1 tsp ground cumin
- 1/2 tsp salt
- 1/8 tsp black pepper

1. **Prep Work One: Chopping**
   Chop carrots.

2. Chop onion, basil, thyme, and garlic and set aside in a bowl.

3. Chop eggplant and zucchini, set aside in a bowl.

4. Drain and press tofu as described in *Common Food Prep Technique Tips, Step Seven* and set aside.

5. Chop tomato and leave on cutting board.

**Prep Work Two: Assemble in Large Cook-pot.**

1. Add 2-3 tsp grape seed or avocado oil to cooking pot and add chopped carrots. Sauté for 5 minutes.

2. Add chopped onion, basil, thyme, and garlic and sauté 3 minutes.

3. Add chopped eggplant and zucchini; crumble big chunks of tofu into pot; and sauté for 3 minutes.

4. Add chopped tomato, all tomato sauce, and pesto to the pot. Bring to a boil. Then reduce to simmer for 30 minutes.

5. Stir mixture occasionally through cooking period. Then remove from heat and stir in cumin, salt, and pepper.

**Asparagus Orange Quinoa with Pecans**

**(A favorite recipe inspired by "Cooking Light Magazine", April 2008, with Dena's Twist and Food Prep Tips)**

- **1 tsp coconut oil**
- **1/2 cup white onion, chopped fine**
- **2 tbsp minced red onion**
- **1 cup quinoa**
- **1/2 tsp salt**
- **2 cups of water**
- **1/2 pound asparagus, chopped**
- **1/4 cup pecans, toasted**
- **1 cup of small orange sections (use mandarins, satsumas, or clementines)**
- **5 medjool dates, pitted and chopped**
- **1/4 -1/2 jalapeno pepper, diced**
- **Dressing:**
- **2 tbsp lemon or lime juice**
- **1 tbsp hemp oil**
- **1/4 tsp salt and pepper each**
- **2 garlic cloves, minced**
- **2 tbsp fresh mint, chopped**

**Prep Work One: Preheat and Cook Quinoa**

1. Preheat oven to 350° (in preparation for Prep Two).

2. Place coconut oil in a large kettle and heat on low. Chop white onion and place in oil. Sauté for 2 minutes.

3. While white onions are cooking, chop red onion and place in a large salad bowl.

4. Add quinoa to cooking white onions after 2 minutes and sauté for 5 minutes.

5. Add 2 cups of water and salt to quinoa, and bring to a boil.

6. Reduce to simmer, cover, and cook for 15 minutes.

7. Chop asparagus and add to quinoa when five minutes remain in cooking process (at 10 minutes).

8. Remove from heat and let stand for 10 minutes.

### Prep Work Two: While Quinoa Is Cooking, Roast Pecans.

1. Place pecans (not chopped) on a rimmed baking sheet and bake 5-10 minutes in preheated oven. Check frequently and mix as needed to prevent burning.

2. Set aside, then chop slightly (totaling 1/4 cup), and add to large salad bowl containing chopped red onions.

### Prep Work Three: Make Dressing and Finish Salad Mix

1. Place all dressing ingredients (except mint) in a large coffee mug and whisk until combined.

2. Add orange slices, dates, and jalapeno to the large salad bowl containing red onions and pecans. Gently combine.

3. When quinoa/asparagus mixture has cooled slightly, add to bowl and mix.

4. Pour dressing over salad bowl mixture and gently mix. Place quinoa salad onto individual plates and top with chopped mint.

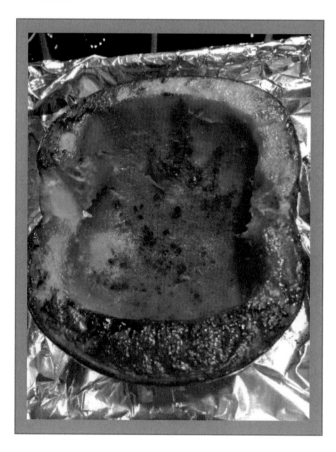

### Acorn Squash Stuffed with Cannellini Beans, Farro, and Dried Cherries

**(A favorite recipe adapted from "Health Magazine", December 2016, with Dena's Food Prep Tips)**

- 3 acorn squash
- 1 cup farro, uncooked
- 3 cups water
- 1/2 cup hazelnuts, toasted and chopped
- 1/2 cup dried cherries, chopped
- 2 tbsp olive or avocado oil
- 1 cup yellow onion, chopped
- 1/2 cup celery, finely chopped
- 1/2 cup carrot, finely chopped
- 1 tbsp fresh sage, chopped
- 15 oz can of Cannellini (white) beans, drained and rinsed
- 1 1/2 tsp salt
- 1 tsp pepper

### Prep Work One: Prepare/Cook Squash

1. Preheat oven to 350°

2. Cut squash in half lengthwise. Scoop out and discard seeds.

3. Place squash cut-side up on a large rimmed baking sheet lined with parchment paper.

4. Rub a small amount of coconut oil on the insides of each cut squash, and sprinkle with salt and pepper.

5. Place in oven and bake for 45 minutes.

### Prep Work Two: Roast Hazelnuts

1. Place nuts in a baking pan so all in one layer. Bake for 10-15 minutes (in same pre-heated oven cooking squash) until skins are slightly blistered.

2. Remove from the oven and wrap in a dish towel for 1 minute. Then rub in towel to loosen skins and remove towel and skins.

### Prep Work Three: Cook Farro

1. Rinse farro. Then add 1 cup farro to 3 cups of water in a medium-sized kettle and bring to a boil.

2. Turn down to simmer and cover, cooking for 25-30 minutes until water is absorbed. This should make more than 2 cups cooked farro, so save the extra for a lunch or dinner protein source the following day.

3. After 20 minutes of cooking, add chopped cherries, mix, and complete farro cooking time.

**Prep Work Four: Chop and Cook Vegetables**

1. While squash and farro are cooking, chop cherries and set aside. (After 20 minutes of farro cooking, add chopped cherries.)

2. Chop onion, celery, and carrot, and place in a large skillet with 1–2 tbsp olive oil over medium heat for 10 minutes.

3. Add chopped sage, stir for 1 minute, and remove from heat.

4. Stir in cooked farro, canned beans, hazelnuts, 3/4 tsp salt, and 1/2 tsp pepper.

**Prep Work Five: Fill Squash and Final Cooking**

1. Spoon farro mixture evenly into cooked squash halves.

2. Drizzle with small amount of olive or avocado oil, return to oven, and bake 10-15 minutes or until filling is slightly browned.

**Black Bean Enchiladas with Zucchini and Corn**

**(A favorite recipe inspired by "Cooking Light Magazine", May 2007, with Dena's Twist and Food Prep Tips)**

**Sauce (make a day in advance and store in refrigerator for best flavor):**
- **1/2 cup red onion, diced**
- **2 tsp garlic, minced**
- **1 tsp grapeseed oil**
- **1/2 cup vegetable broth (or water)**
- **1 can (28-ounce) crushed tomatoes plus liquid**
- **1 tbsp honey**
- **1 tbsp chili powder**
- **1 tsp cumin**
- **1/2 tsp salt**

1. Chop onion and mince garlic. Add to large saucepan with heated oil and sauté on medium heat for 5 minutes.

2. Slowly add in the broth and mix in onion and garlic. Add ingredients tomatoes through salt and mix, bring to a low boil, then lower to simmer, and cook for 30 minutes.

3. If making in advance, let sauce cool, then store in a glass container, and refrigerate.

**Filling:**
- **2 cups zucchini, diced**
- **1 package (10 ounce) frozen white corn**
- **1 tsp grape seed oil**
- **1 can (15 ounce) black beans, rinsed and drained**
- **1 1/2 cups of fresh spinach (chopped)**
- **2 cups shredded vegan cheese (optional)**
- **whole wheat tortillas**

1. Preheat oven to 350°.

2. Chop zucchini, rinse and drain black beans, chop spinach, and set aside.

3. Heat oil in a large skillet over medium heat, add chopped zucchini and corn, sauté for 5 minutes, then stir in beans, turn off heat, and set aside.

4. Lightly coat a 13 X 9-inch baking dish with coconut oil. Spread about 1 cup of the sauce on the bottom of the baking dish.

**Fill Tortillas:**

1. Place individual tortillas on a flat surface (a cutting board works well) and scoop 1/2 cup of zucchini/corn mixture down the center of a tortilla.

2. Lightly sprinkle with chopped spinach (don't over fill), sprinkle lightly with vegan cheese if using, and roll up.

3. Place in the baking dish, seam-side down, and repeat for the remaining tortillas.

4. Once all tortillas are rolled and placed in the baking dish, spread 2 cups of sauce on top.

5. Cover baking dish with foil and bake for 30 minutes.

6.  Pull out of the oven, uncover, and sprinkle with remaining vegan cheese, if using, and bake for 10 additional minutes.

### Dessert Choices

The raw carrot cake with pistachios shown below is an example of elaborate desserts that are plant-based. In contrast, the recipes provided for you in this section are simple and satisfying. Once you get a taste for these simpler treats, the plant-based techniques used to make them, and the nutritional substitutions for unhealthy standard dessert ingredients, you will be set to make this carrot cake and other more complicated delicacies. Such delicacies will be featured in the next edition:

**Dena's Fuel For Fitness**

**"pleas'n every vegan"**

**Phase Two: Advanced Plant-Based Lifestyle**

### Cherry Chia Raw Crumble (page 81, top right)

**(A favorite recipe adapted from wholefoodsmarket.com with Dena's Food Prep Tips)**

- 7-8 cups fresh cherries, pitted and quartered
- 1 tsp orange zest
- 3 tbsp orange juice from one orange
- 1 cup medjool dates, pitted and chopped
- 1/2 tsp vanilla
- 3/4 cup slivered almonds
- 1/3 cup chia seeds
- 2 tsp cinnamon
- 1/2 tsp clove

### Prep Work One: Chop and Juice

1.  Chop cherries into quarters and place in a medium-sized bowl.
2.  Chop dates and place in food processor.
3.  Wash the orange, zest with microplane for 1 tsp, and place in food processor. Juice the orange totaling 3 tbsp. Set both aside.

### Prep Work Two: Cherry Filling

Add vanilla and 2 tbsp orange juice (keep 1 tbsp for the topping) to bowl of cherries and mix. Spoon the mixture evenly into an 8-inch square baking dish.

### Prep Work Three: Topping

1.  Add almonds, chia, cinnamon, and clove to food processor containing dates. Process until mixture still has some texture but is well mixed.
2.  Add remaining 1 tbsp orange juice and pulse until combined.
3.  Place chunks of the mixture on top of the cherries in the baking dish. Use your fingers to ensure evenly distributed.
4.  The crumble can be refrigerated for 2-3 days or eaten right away.

### Tahini Cashew Cacao Brownies

**(A favorite recipe inspired by vegan blogger Sina, of veganheaven.org with Dena's Twist and Food Prep Tips)**

- 1 flax egg
- 2 1/2 tbsp melted coconut oil
- 3 tbsp applesauce
- 2 cups of spelt flour
- 1 cup almond milk
- 1/2 cup maple syrup
- 3/4 cup cacao powder
- 2 tsp baking powder
- 1 tsp vanilla

- **1/2 cup vegan chocolate chips**
- **1/2 cup tahini**

**Topping:**

- **2 tbsp tahini**
- **1/4 cup cashews**
- **1/2 cup dark chocolate, melted**

**Prep Work One: Flax Egg**

1. Preheat oven to 350°
2. Make flax egg by adding 1 tbsp flaxseed meal to 3 tbsp of water, mix, and set aside.

**Prep Work Two: Liquify Coconut Oil**

1. If coconut oil is solid, place a small amount in a coffee mug and microwave for 15 seconds or until a liquid consistency.
2. Measure out 2 1/2 tbsp. and place in a large mixing bowl. Use extra oil to lightly grease the 8-inch X 10-inch baking pan to be used for baking the brownies.

**Prep Work Three: Make Apple Sauce**

1. If you don't want to use store bought applesauce (may have excess sugar and preservatives), just place chunks of peeled and chopped apple in the food processor and mix until you get the consistency of applesauce.
2. For extra flavor, follow instructions for Roasted Apples in the recipe, *Pumpkin Apple Muffins* found in the Breakfast Section and make applesauce.
3. Measure out 3 tbsp applesauce and add to the mixing bowl.

**Prep Work Four: Make Batter**

Add the flour and ingredients through tahini, plus the previously mixed flax egg, to the large mixing bowl and combine all brownie ingredients. Pour the batter into the oiled 8-inch X 10-inch baking pan.

**Prep Work Five: Make Topping and Chocolate Drizzle**

1. Drizzle the 2 tbsp tahini over the batter and use the tip of a butter knife to swirl the tahini without mixing it into the batter.
2. Sprinkle the cashews evenly over the tahini swirl and bake in the oven for 25-28 minutes.

Insert a toothpick into the cooked brownies, and if it comes out clean (without uncooked batter sticking to it) it's done and can be removed from the oven and set aside to cool.

3. Once the brownies have cooled, melt the chocolate in a coffee mug in the microwave and drizzle over the cooled brownies.
4. Cut the brownies into squares and store in a glass container with cover at room temperature or freeze.

## Cacao Walnut Hemp Seed (No-bake) Brownies

**(A favorite recipe adapted from Emily Voneuw, of Thisrawsomeveganlife.com with Dena's Twist and Food Prep Tips)**

**Brownie:**

- **1 cup walnuts, soaked**
- **1 cup garbanzo or oat flour**
- **1/4 cup maple syrup**
- **3 tbsp cacao powder**
- **2 tbsp coconut oil, melted**
- **2 tbsp hemp seed**
- **1 tbsp chia seeds**
- **1 tsp vanilla**
- **1/8 tsp salt**

**Frosting:**

- **2 tbsp coconut oil, melted**
- **2 tbsp maple syrup**
- **2 tbsp cacao powder**

**Toppings:**

- **1 tbsp hemp seeds**
- **1-2 tbsp shredded coconut**
- **1-2 tbsp vegan chocolate chips or cacao nibs**

### Prep Work One: Soak Walnuts

Soak walnuts for 30 minutes to one hour. Then discard soaking liquid.

### Prep Work Two: Liquify Coconut Oil

If coconut oil is solid, place a small amount in a coffee mug and microwave for 15 seconds or until a liquid consistency. Measure out 2 tbsp for the batter. Reserve 2 tbsp in a small bowl for the frosting.

### Prep Work Three: Make the Batter

1. Place all ingredients into the food processor and mix until smooth and all ingredients come together into a large ball.
2. Place parchment paper into an 8-inch X 10-inch baking pan, and using your fingertips, press the brownie mixture evenly into the pan.
3. Place pan in the refrigerator for 1-2 hours until firm.

### Prep Work Four: Make the Frosting

1. Once the brownies are firm, make the frosting. In the small bowl with previously reserved coconut oil, mix remaining frosting ingredients with a spoon until they form a smooth frosting.
2. Remove the brownies from the refrigerator, pour the frosting over the top of the brownies, and sprinkle the toppings of your choice on top. You are going to want to add those chocolate chips or cacao nibs.
3. Return the baking pan to the refrigerator, allowing the frosting to harden (at least an hour). Then go for it! I also like to store these brownies in the freezer. They're a super delicious treat when semi-frozen!

## Salted Cashew Maca Tahini Squares

**(A favorite recipe from Ella Mills, of *Deliously Ella* and author of *Natural Feasts* with Dena's Food Prep Tips)**

- **1 1/2 cups raw cashews**
- **2 tsp vanilla**
- **6 medjool dates, pitted and chopped**
- **3 tbsp coconut sugar**
- **3 tbsp tahini**
- **2 tbsp maca powder**

1. Add cashews and vanilla to a food processor and mix for 3-4 minutes until nut pieces are finely ground, but not creamy (don't want nuts to release oils).
2. Add chopped dates, coconut sugar, tahini, and maca, and process until smooth.
3. Line a loaf pan with parchment paper, and using your hands, evenly distribute the mixture in the pan.
4. Even out the top of the mixture and sprinkle Himalayan sea salt over the top, gently pressing the salt into the mixture with your fingers.
5. Using a sharp knife, cut into squares and place the pan in the freezer for several hours.
6. When removing the squares from the pan, just pull the parchment paper out of the pan

and peel the squares off the paper. Then store in a glass container in the freezer as a "go to" treat whenever you need one.

## Garbanzo Protein Chocolate Cookies

**(A favorite recipe inspired by Emily Voneuw, of Thisrawsomeveganlife.com with Dena's Twist and Food Prep Tips)**

**Cookie Batter Ingredients:**

- **2 cups garbanzo beans (15-16 oz can), drained and rinsed**
- **1/2 cup Dena's Power Nut/Seed Butter or tahini**
- **1/4 cup spelt or oat flour**
- **1/4 cup maple syrup**
- **1 scoop vegan protein powder (2-3 tbsp)**
- **2 tbsp flaxseed meal**
- **1 tsp baking powder**
- **1 tsp vanilla**
- **1/8 tsp Himalayan sea salt**
- **Vegan chocolate chips or homemade chocolate chunks (see recipe)**

**Chocolate Chunks:**

- **1/4 cup cacao butter**
- **3 tbsp cacao powder**
- **1 tbsp maple syrup**
- **1 tsp tsp vanilla**

**Prep Work One: Make Chocolate Chunks**

1. Preheat oven to 350°
2. Melt cacao butter in a medium saucepan over medium-low heat until liquifies.
3. Mix in remaining ingredients.
4. Place a sheet of parchment paper on a plate and pour warm chocolate mixture onto plate (the smaller the plate, the thicker the final product of hardened chunks).
5. Place plate in the freezer for at least one hour or until the chocolate has hardened.
6. When the cookie dough batter is ready, take the chocolate plate from the freezer, separate the parchment paper from the chocolate and using your hands, and break the chocolate into chunks (a bit larger than chocolate chips).

**Prep Work Two: Make Dena's Power Nut/Seed Butter**

Follow recipe instructions for making Dena's Power Nut/Seed Butter in the Breakfast Section and reserve a 1/2 cup for the cookie batter.

**Prep Work Three: Make Cookie Batter**

1. Place all cookie batter ingredients, except chocolate, into a food processor and mix until creamy.
2. Hand mix in the chocolate chunks from the freezer (or chocolate chips, if using).
3. Scoop a tablespoon of dough onto a non-stick cookie sheet and use your fingertips to flatten each dough ball into the shape of a small round cookie.
4. Bake 20-25 minutes, let cookies cool, and remove from the sheet. Can be stored in the freezer, ready for you to indulge in a refreshing, protein-packed treat!

4. Using your fingertips (lightly moistened with water), separate a small amount of date mixture from the large ball in the processor and roll into a smaller ball in-between the palms of your hands. Try to keep it about half the size of a golf ball. Then place it in the coconut bowl and roll in coconut.

5. Once the ball is evenly coated with coconut, place in a covered glass container for storage in the freezer.

6. Repeat this process for each ball until all of the mixture is gone. To avoid stickiness in the rolling process, periodically lightly moisten your fingertips with water.

## Almond Date Balls Rolled in Coconut (Raw Dessert)

- **1 cup of raw almonds**
- **3 cups medjool dates, pitted and chopped**
- **Shredded coconut for rolling**

1. Place almonds in a food processor and mix until you get a powdery consistency.

2. Chop dates into small pieces and distribute evenly throughout processor bowl containing almonds. Blend until the entire mixture combines into a large ball swirling in the processor.

3. In a small bowl, place about a 1/4 cup of shredded coconut (if need more, add a small amount at a time for rolling).

## Nanacream (Banana-based, Non-dairy Vegan Ice Cream)

- **3-4 ripe bananas, frozen in bite sized pieces**
- **Fruit of choice, best if fresh but can use frozen (blueberries, raspberries, blackberries, cherries, chopped peaches)**

- **Spice of choice (cinnamon, cardamom, clove, nutmeg, pumpkin pie spice)**

1. Place fruit of choice in the Vitamix. If using frozen fruit, allow to thaw slightly for 5-10 minutes.

2. Sprinkle spice (1 tbsp of a spice or combination).

3. Remove pre-frozen bananas from the freezer, break off bite-sized pieces to equal 3-4 medium-sized bananas, and place in a Vitamix. (Don't try with other blenders unless they have equivalent strength to the Vitamix.) Allow the banana to unthaw/soften slightly 2–3 minutes.

4. Place the lid on the Vitamix and make sure it is secure and snapped into place.

5. Twist and lift from the lid the clear lid plug and insert the Tamper (shown at top right) through the lid opening. As long as the lid is secured in place, it will ensure that the Tamper does not reach the bottom of the Vitamix and does not come in contact with the blades.

6. Double check that the lid is locked in place with the Tamper inserted, stabilize the Vitamix container by holding the handle (without pushing it down into the machine), turn the Vitamix on low, and using your dominant hand, move the tamper up and down to help grind the frozen mixture around. You may have to turn the Vitamix off (so as not to burn up the motor) and continue to mix with the tamper. (Do not remove the lid.) Turn the unit back on low, and grind a bit more. You want to complete this in about 40 seconds to one-minute total time so you don't completely melt your nanacream as it heats up in the unit. Turn the unit off, remove the container from the motor unit, and remove the Tamper and the lid.

7. Immediately scoop out your nanacream into bowls and eat right away! I like it with chunks of berries still visible, which adds great texture to this non-dairy vegan ice cream!

As you make many nanacream varieties, you will establish the thickness, and fruit/spice

combinations that are your favorites. Don't limit yourself to the options I have listed. Be creative and generate your own combinations. Great summer treats!

**Apple Raisin Pie (Raw Dessert)**

(One of my favorite recipes by Ani Phyo in "Ani's Raw Food Kitchen" with Dena's Food Prep Tips)

**Crust:**

- 2 cups almonds, raw
- 1 tsp Himalayan sea salt
- 2 cups dates, chopped

**Syrup for Pie Filling:**

- 1/2 cup dates, chopped
- 1 orange, chopped

**Apple Filling:**

- 5 cups apples, peeled, thinly sliced
- 1 cup raisins
- 2 tbsp cinnamon

**Prep Work One: Chop/Slice and Peel**

1. Chop dates, place 2 cups in a medium bowl, and place 1/2 cup dates in a small bowl.
2. Peel one orange, chop into bite-sized pieces, and place in the small bowl with 1/2 cup dates.
3. Peel about 5-6 apples, slice thinly, place in a large bowl, add raisins and cinnamon, and mix gently without damaging the apple slices.
4. Then set all bowls aside.

**Prep Work Two: Make the Pie Crust**

1. Add 2 cups of almonds to the processor and chop into small pieces, with some portions ground into a small amount of powder. (Don't over process.)
2. Spread a small amount of the powder on the bottom of an 8" or 9" pie plate with removable bottom (the smaller the pie plate, the higher you will pile the apples in the plate).
3. Then add to the processor 2 cups of chopped dates and mix with almonds until the mixture forms a ball (the pie crust).
4. Using a metal spoon, pull out small portions of the crust from the processor and press the into the pie plate using your fingers, starting on the bottom and adding crust up along the sides until all crust has been placed in the pie plate. Then set aside the pie plate.

**Prep Work Three: Make Syrup for Pie Filling**

Without rinsing the processor bowl, put the chopped oranges and 1/2 cup dates into the processor and blend until the mixture becomes a thick liquid or syrup.

**Prep Work Four: Assemble the Pie**

1. Add the syrup from the food processor to the bowl of apple slices and raisins and toss again gently.

2. Spoon the apple mixture into the pie crust, piling the apples high, arranging with your fingers to fit in the crust.

3. Store in the refrigerator at least an hour for the crust to set. Prior to cutting slices of pie, lift the pie tin and gently push the removable bottom up, releasing the pie from the sides of the tin, exposing the crust for easy slicing. The pie will keep for two to three days in the refrigerator.

## Recipe Contributors

- *Ani's Raw Food Kitchen, Ani's Raw Food Desserts, Ani's Raw Food Asia* by Ani Phyo
- *Becoming Vegan* by Brenda Davis & Vesanto Melina
- Cleanfooddirtygirl.com, Molly Patrick
- Deliciouslyella.com, Ella Mills
- Eco Chef, Bryan Au
- Fatfreevegan.com, Susan Voisin
- Fullyraw.com, Kristina Carrillo-Bucaram
- Simplyquinoa.com, Alyssa Rimmer
- *Superfood Kitchen, Superfood Smoothies* by Julie Morris
- *The Raw Food Healing Bible* by Christine Bailey
- *The Raw Food Revolution Diet* by Cherie Soria, Brenda Davis, Vesanto Melina
- *The Raw Gourmet* by Nomi Shannon
- Thisrawsomeveganlife.com, Emily Voneuw
- *Vegan Fusion World Cuisine* by Mark Reinfeld, Bo Rinaldi
- Veganheaven.org, Sina
- *Veganomicon,* by Isa Chandra Moskowitz & Terry Hope Romero
- *Vegetarian Times Magazine*

**Additional Social Media Vegan Favorites on Instagram**

- Buddha Belly Wellness
- Indigo Vegan
- Kimberly Snyder (The Glowing Green Smoothie)
- Lee Supercharged (Lee Holmes)
- Lena's Vegan Living
- Nadia's Healthy Kitchen
- Papaya Sunshine
- Raw Vana (Yovana Mendoza)
- The Minimalist Vegan
- The Raw Boy
- Vegan Feast Catering (Janet Hudson)
- Vegan Heaven

# Step Five: Month One Meal Plan for the Plant-Based Conversion

Depending on the amount of processed, fast, and high sugar foods you have been consuming, this will help you determine the amount of time it will take for your taste buds and digestion to get used to the new healthy lifestyle. You can start slowly by incorporating one meal or snack daily for the first week and gradually add an additional meal or snack for the next three weeks. You should then be ready to start your first full Weekly Menu.

Every person has a large number of factors—level of fitness, family versus individual meal responsibilities, health complications, monetary and time restrictions, to name a few—that would make it impossible to make hard and fast rules about when and what to eat. This is not a book to instruct you to eat exactly three meals a day, to tell you what time to eat your meals, or how often you should be consuming snacks. This is a wonderfully flexible lifestyle, and as long as you fulfill your daily requirements, you can build a daily schedule that works for your life.

Some days you will want or need to eat breakfast. Other days your body will tell you to eat a combined breakfast/lunch at 11:00 AM. Some people choose to eat their largest meal at lunchtime, while others do so at dinner. That is why there is not a separate lunch and dinner menu section in the Recipe Library. There will be times when you would rather combine several snacks to make a nutritious dinner rather than prepare a specific meal. The great thing about this book and my plan is that you can do that because all of the snacks are from whole foods and contribute to quality nutrition.

Overall, this book will tell you *what to eat* when you are ready to fuel your body. So, as you look at the suggested recipes for Month One Meal Planning, although there are items listed under breakfast, lunch, snack, dinner, and dessert, it doesn't mean you need to eat each one of those items. If you are taking a fitness day off, back off on the snack or dessert item, or if you just aren't hungry in the evening, substitute the dinner meal for one of the nutritious snacks. This section is designed to provide you with a general guide, but each person's schedule and appetite will vary, so focus on finding the combinations that work best for you.

In addition to listening to your body to determine when to fuel it, your organizational skills will greatly affect your success in becoming plant-based. If you use an iphone, daily planner, or other organizational device, you will need to schedule every Sunday a time slot to plan your weekly menu (Step Five), shopping time (Step Six), and food prep time (Step Seven). This section will concentrate on planning the weekly menu. As you move through this task on a weekly basis, you will get more efficient at this, so don't get discouraged if the first two weeks take extra time to plan the menu. I suggest doing this on a Sunday, but if your schedule works better on another day of the week, pick the day that fits your schedule best.

The weekly menu plan will consist of six days instead of seven because research shows that most people want to eat out at least one night per week, and/or for various reasons, most people have at least one night during the week where all they need is a "light" evening meal

that may consist of leftovers or a simple meal such as a salad topped with a protein source. It is not necessary to make a big "production" every night when you are deciding what to eat. Just keep it simple, but balanced, and you will not only enjoy the plant-based lifestyle, but you will stick with it.

The majority of this section provides you with the initial month of meals (all from recipes found in Step Four) to introduce you to the world of plant-based living while ensuring that you get plenty of variety in flavor while maintaining nutritional balance. For the second month and remaining months on the plant-based jump start program, you can either repeat the menus from month one, or plan your own meals from the recipe list. When you are ready to create your own Meal Plan, you will quickly discover that there are multiple combinations for the simpler dishes (e.g., roasted vegetables paired with a grain, or salad and dressing choices) that not only keep you and your taste buds interested in each meal but it also ensure you will be consuming a variety of nutrients.

## Month One Meal Plan for the Plant-Based Jump Start Program

Remember these are guidelines. You can eat unlimited fruit and greens if you are still hungry. There are also numerous choices in the protein category (nuts, seeds, lentils, beans, tempeh). Try to reach only occasionally for a handful of store bought crackers or a slice of whole wheat toast as add-ons to the menu items. Your ultimate goal is to eat more greens, veggies, plant-based protein, nuts/seeds, or fruit.

## Guidelines for Creating Your Customized Weekly Meal Plan

After following the first month's Meal Plan you should have a better feel for the types of plant-based foods you like, when you need to fuel your body, and the amount of food you need to sustain your level of daily activity. Don't limit yourself to the recipes provided in this book. Explore plant-based cookbooks, websites, Instagram feeds, and blogs to expand your own recipe library.

| Week One | Breakfast | Snack optional | Lunch | Snack optional | Dinner | Dessert optional |
|---|---|---|---|---|---|---|
| Sunday | Pumpkin muffin | | Green salad* w/lentil cashew dressing | Fruit with ¼ cup granola | Asparagus Orange Quinoa w/ pecans and Apricot Beet Salad w/apples | Walnut stuffed dates (2) |
| Monday | Fruit bowl with nuts, seeds, dried fruit | Almond Coconut Cranberry Bar | Apricot Beet Salad w/apples (leftovers) | | Green Dinner Salad* w/lentil cashew dressing and side of black bean, onion, avocado | Nanacream or Non-dairy yogurt |
| Tuesday | Smoothie (Green with protein powder) | | Rice Cakes topped w/black beans and avocado (leftovers) side of carrots and fruit, Green smoothie (if extra from breakfast) | Walnut stuffed dates (2) | Tofu Scramble w/veggies and greens w/ Creamy Mustard Dressing (optional wheat toast with nut butter) | Pumpkin muffin |
| Wednesday | Oatmeal w/ nuts, dried fruit | | Multi-grain sandwich bread with Creamy Mustard Dressing, mashed garbanzo, shredded carrots, red onion | Apple with 2 tbsp nut butter | Carrot Curry Soup and green salad (add ½ can garbanzo stored in refrig) w/avocado mango pistachio dressing | Almond Coconut Cranberry Bar |
| Thursday | Pumpkin muffin | Banana Slices with tahini, cacao nibs | Carrot Curry Soup and small green salad w/avocado mango pistachio dressing (leftovers) | | Pinto Bean Basil Dip with crudité and stir-fry tempeh with red pepper and mushrooms on a bed of spinach | Fruit or Nanacream |
| Friday | Non-dairy Yogurt and Fruit | | Romaine wraps with Pinto Bean Basil dip, chopped spinach, veggies | Rice Cakes w/ avocado | Dinner Out | |
| Saturday | Smoothie | Almond Coconut Cranberry Bar | Honeydew and Cucumber Soup | | Wheatberry Salad w/Raisins | Garbanzo Protein Chocolate Cookies |

*choose your favorite vegetables: steam, stir-fry, roast, or add raw

| Week Two | Breakfast | Snack optional | Lunch | Snack optional | Dinner | Dessert optional |
|---|---|---|---|---|---|---|
| Sunday | Greens and Fruit | | Wheatberry Salad w/Raisins (leftovers) | | Black Bean Enchiladas with Zucchini and Corn | Cacao Chia Bar |
| Monday | Dairy-free Yogurt and Fruit | | Black Bean Enchiladas with Zucchini and Corn (leftovers) | ¼-½ cup granola, kiwi and orange | Quinoa Salad with Cilantro Pesto | Garbanzo Protein Chocolate Cookies |
| Tuesday | Millet with toppings | Walnut Stuffed dates (2) | Quinoa Salad (leftovers) with Carrot sticks | | Lentils with steamed or roasted veggies* w/Asian Dressing | Cantaloupe Slices |
| Wednesday | Smoothie | | Coconut wrap filled with lentils and veggies with Asian dressing (leftovers) | Cantaloupe Slices | Green Dinner Salad* Strawberry Hemp Dressing and Hummus on crackers | Almond Coconut Cranberry Bar |

# 90 — Month One Meal Plan

| | | | | | | |
|---|---|---|---|---|---|---|
| **Thursday** | Greens and Fruit with Strawberry Hemp Dressing | Pumpkin muffin | Sesame Oil, Cucumber and Miso Dish and chopped apple and berries with Granola | | Cauliflower Quinoa Hummus Soup with whole grain toast topped with avocado | Cacao Chia Bar |
| **Friday** | Green Smoothie | | Black Bean, red onion, and avocado on rice cakes and Cauliflower Quinoa Hummus Soup (leftovers) | Almond Coconut Cranberry Bar | Orange Sunflower Slaw and Tahini Roasted Broccoli | Fruit |
| **Saturday** | Chlorella Banana Bowl | | Apricot Beet Salad with Apples and Dairy-Free Yogurt | Seaweed Snacks with Avocado | Dinner Out | Healthy Dessert after dinner or fruit |

*choose your favorite vegetables: steam, stir-fry, roast, or add raw

| **Week Three** | **Breakfast** | **Snack** optional | **Lunch** | **Snack** optional | **Dinner** | **Dessert** optional |
|---|---|---|---|---|---|---|
| **Sunday** | Oatmeal | | Apricot Beet Salad (leftovers) | Granola | Ratatouille w/tofu | Apricot Hemp Square |
| **Monday** | Wheatgerm Flax with Cranberry Muffin | | Ratatouille w/tofu (leftovers) | Seaweed Snacks with avocado | Salad* with Hemp Seed Brazil Nut Dressing and Pea Dill Soup | Cacao Pistachio Chia Bar |
| **Tuesday** | Greens and Fruit | | Pea Dill Soup (leftovers) and chopped apple, dried figs, and walnuts | Almond Date Balls | Faro with Red Pepper and Snow Peas | Apricot Hemp Squares |
| **Wednesday** | Smoothie - Green | | Faro with Red Pepper (leftovers) and Wheatgerm Flax with Cranberry Muffin | Pear and Banana | Tempeh with steamed veggies on a bed of greens | Nanacream |
| **Thursday** | Greens and Fruit | | Black bean, onion avocado sandwich on whole grain bread | Apricot Hemp Squares | Asparagus Orange Quinoa with Pecans, Grape Almond Soup | Almond Date Balls |
| **Friday** | Wheatgerm Flax with Cranberry Muffin | Walnut Stuffed dates | Asparagus Quinoa, Chopped melon with dried cranberries | | Dinner Out | Healthy Dessert after dinner or fruit |
| **Saturday** | Smoothie | | Papaya Avocado with Mixed Greens | Rice Cakes top with nut butter or tahini | Quinoa Salad with Cilantro Pesto | Apple Raisin Pie |

*choose your favorite vegetables: steam, stir-fry, roast, or add raw

| **Week Four** | **Breakfast** | **Snack** optional | **Lunch** | **Snack** optional | **Dinner** | **Dessert** optional |
|---|---|---|---|---|---|---|
| **Sunday** | Oatmeal | Seaweed Snacks | Quinoa Salad with Cilantro Pesto (leftovers) | | Acorn Squash stuffed with Cannellini Beans, Farro and Dried Cherries | Apple Raisin Pie |
| **Monday** | Fruit with chopped dates, nuts and seeds | | Acorn Squash (leftovers) | Apple Raisin Pie | Tofu Scramble w/veggies* over spinach | Cacao Walnut Hempseed Brownies |
| **Tuesday** | Smoothie | | Greens and Fruit | Salted Cashew Maca Tahini Squares | Carrot Curry Soup w/ green salad* Avocado Toast | Apricot Hemp Square |

| | | | | | | |
|---|---|---|---|---|---|---|
| **Wednesday** | Yogurt and Fruit | Rice Cakes with hummus or avocado | Carrot Curry Soup (leftovers) and Chickpea Sandwich | | Quinoa and Red Pepper w/ Strawberry Hemp Dressing and Macadamia and Sun-Dried Tomato Spread w/ crudité | Apple Raisin Pie |
| **Thursday** | Smoothie | | Quinoa and Red Pepper (leftovers) | Macadamia and Sun-Dried Tomato Spread on crackers | Cabbage Carrot Cucumber Slaw w/ Ginger Orange Tahini | Cacao Walnut Hempseed Brownies |
| **Friday** | Chlorella Banana Bowl | | Black bean, onion avocado salad | Granola with fruit | Roasted Cauliflower with Tahini and Garlic and Lentils, Blueberry Beet and Walnut Salad | Salted Cashew Maca Tahini Squares |
| **Saturday** | Smoothie | | Blueberry Beet Salad (leftovers) | Salted Cashew Maca Tahini Squares | Dinner Out | Healthy Dessert after dinner or fruit |

*choose your favorite vegetables: steam, stir-fry, roast, or add raw

You should be planning to eat your daily calculated protein requirement (instructions for calculation in the Introduction section, *What do I need to know about proteins?*). Some people like to eat all of their protein for the day at one meal, but I suggest you spread it out throughout the day, not only at mealtime, but with the plant-based lifestyle, your snacks are also great protein sources.

Be mindful to incorporate different foods throughout the week (e,g., don't eat the same foods for lunch every day) to ensure you are eating a variety of nutrients. A good guide is to eat a variety of colors with your fruits and vegetables which deliver different nutrients. Check out the hashtag on Instagram, #eattherainbow.

One of the most important transitions to make sure you incorporate into your daily meal planning is to increase your consumption of Greens. The nutrients and disease prevention support these foods provide (see the Greens Table in Step Two) can't be understated. Your ultimate goal should be to consume Greens as 50-80% of your overall daily intake. That can be in the form of leafy greens, green vegetables, smoothies, juices, soups, green fruits (kiwi, grapes, melons)... Eat them up! Just plan your meals as much as you can around the foundation of Greens and you will be good to go.

The plant-based lifestyle is also mindful of food waste, so try to clear out all the fruit and veggies in your refrigerator or on your countertop before buying more. This task will also help you decide what to put in that Tofu Scramble when you can't decide which veggies you want to add or what flavor smoothie you should blend. Using this technique, I have come up with some fantastic flavor combinations I never would have tried that have become some of my all-time favorites.

## Step Six: How to Develop Weekly Shopping Lists That Match the Weekly Menu

Prior to starting the first month, order the following items online or purchase them from a gourmet grocery store:

- **Raw granola** (favorite brand—Living Intentions, activated superfood cereal, found online at livingintentions.com and Amazon.) Try the following varieties: Hemp and Greens or Blueberry Blast.

- **Protein Powder** (non-whey/dairy protein products. Favorite vegan brand is Billy's Infinity Protein, found online at infinitygreens.com and Amazon.)

- **Chlorella,** a detoxifying supplement and a source of chlorophyll, it contains the following essential nutrients: protein, iron, magnesium, and amino acids. Chlorella is able to bind to heavy metals and toxic chemicals in the body. (Found online at favorite suppliers: Ultimate Superfoods, Navitas, and gourmet grocery stores.) Despite the similarities between chlorella and spirulina, my personal preference is chlorella due to a milder flavor, and it's richer in chlorophyll, but they can be used interchangeably.

- **Hemp Seeds** are the most nutritious seeds in the world—rich in healthy fats (the optimal range of 3:1 omega-6 to omega-3 fatty acids), rich in protein (2-3 tablespoons hemp seeds provide about 11 grams of protein), a complete plant-based protein source (provide all essential amino acids), and a source of various minerals. Look for whole hemp seeds to benefit from the fiber versus shelled hemp seeds (e.g., hemp hearts) which contain very little fiber. (Found online at favorite suppliers: Ultimate Superfoods, Navitas, and gourmet grocery stores.)

- **Cacao**—This is a raw product made by cold-pressing unroasted cocoa beans, which maintains the living enzymes in the cocoa and removes the fat (cacao butter). Cacao is the highest source of antioxidants and magnesium of all foods. Cacao contains four times the antioxidant power of average dark chocolate and more than twenty times than that of blueberries. The difference with cocoa powder is that it has been roasted at high temperatures and often contains added sugars. (Found online at favorite suppliers: Ultimate Superfoods, Navitas, and gourmet grocery stores.)

- **Cacao Nibs**—Cacao beans chopped into tiny pieces that can be sprinkled on foods, like chocolate chips but without added sugars and fats. (Found online at favorite suppliers: Ultimate Superfoods, Navitas, and gourmet grocery stores.)

- **Grains**—Depending on what products are available in your local grocery store, you may have to order some products on-line (farro, wheatberries, millet.)

Once you have planned your menu for the week, it is easy to make your weekly shopping list. Set all of your recipes out in front of you (hard copies or electronic recipes) and simply go through the ingredients in every menu item you have chosen and determine if you already have the item. (Actually go to the pantry, refrigerator, or freezer where you would store the item and check if you have it or are running low.) If you know you have the ingredient, then it doesn't need to go on the list. If your supply of the item is running low, or it's an item you need to replace weekly (like greens and fruits), or you don't have the ingredient, then put it on the list. Make sure you identify the quantity you need in a specific recipe and include the information on the shopping list so you purchase the correct amount and don't come up short while you are actually creating the dish. (E.g., if you are making the raw apple pie and you don't have enough apples, that is really frustrating.) Now that you have your list, determine if you can find everything at one store or if you need to go to multiple locations or place an order online for specialty items.

Instead of saying you will "get to the store" sometime on Sunday, actually schedule the time you plan to go shopping and try to stick as closely as possible to that time frame. Let's say your favorite television series starts at 6:00 PM on Sundays. You better get to the store earlier in the day because your entire healthy upcoming week depends on it, and then you can comfortably enjoy your show too! If you haven't already noticed, much of your success in transitioning to a plant-based diet, or in any many areas of your life, will center around your ability to be organized and plan ahead.

Allow some extra time when you return from your weekly shopping to put groceries away in an orderly way and do some prep work (e.g., place fresh herbs in Mason jars with water). The prep work prolongs freshness and ensures you are getting the highest nutritional value from the items you purchased all the way to the end of the week.

Remember, with all new habits, things get easier and faster the more you practice, and the same is true with your plant-based grocery shopping. Be patient and focus on the long-term benefits. You will see that shopping for a plant-based lifestyle becomes easier and easier.

The first week on the program will be the largest grocery list because you will be purchasing staples (grains, nuts, seeds, dried fruits, spices, oils) that you will be using for weeks and even months to come. Let's take a look at what the shopping list for Week One from the Jump Start Program would look like:

- **Fruits:** apples (6-8), bananas (8-10), oranges (3), avocado (4), mango (2), honeydew melon, cucumbers (3-4), blueberries fresh and frozen,
- **Greens:** romaine (2), spinach-pre-washed (2), kale (2),
- **Vegetables:** asparagus, red beets (2-3), carrots, red onion, garlic, red pepper, broccoli, zucchini, peas (frozen), celery
- **Grains:** oatmeal, quinoa
- Refrigerated items: tofu (2), tempeh (2), lentils (pre-cooked), non-dairy yogurt (2-3), nutmilk
- **Canned Items:** pumpkin, garbanzo beans (3), pinto beans
- **Nuts:** almonds, pistachios, walnuts, cashews, pecans, Brazil nuts, nut butter (optional)
- **Seeds:** pumpkin, sunflower, tahini
- **Dried Fruits:** medjool dates, cranberries, raisins
- **Spices:** curry, pumpkin pie spice, vanilla
- **Herbs:** fresh basil, cilantro, mint
- **Other:** rice cakes, vegan chocolate/chocolate chips, coconut (shredded), multi-grain bread, granola, egg replacer, mustard, coconut sugar, sucanat, grapeseed oil, olive oil, lemon juice, nutritional yeast, honey, flaxseed meal, maple syrup

# Step Seven: Guidelines for Matching Food Prep with the Weekly Meal Plan

Set up either a chalkboard or grease board in your kitchen where you will write the day of the week and corresponding weekly prep work (as listed below). This will keep you organized in your kitchen and on schedule for prepping food for the next day's lunch/dinner or making a batch of snack/energy bars. Whenever you make

snack foods or muffins, place whatever you are not eating that day in a freezer-safe container as you will be consuming these snacks periodically throughout the week, and even into the following week if you have extra items. You should always have on hand extra fruit, avocados, rice cakes, nuts, seeds, dried fruit, and greens to reach for, or pack for work and leave at your desk, to make sure you are ready for extra healthy snacking. As with all new habits, this will become second nature to you in time, but for now, allow yourself the extra time to plan ahead by using either a chalkboard or grease board.

**Weekly Food Prep Schedule for Week One (pre-designated menu from Step Four)**

To start the program, I suggest grocery shopping for the first week on Saturday until you adjust to weekly meal planning, shopping, and prepping food on Sunday. You will see that I suggest your first meal as "morning." While for most people, that will be breakfast and will be consumed before you leave for work, for others who don't like to eat first thing in the morning, this may happen closer to the lunch hour. Be flexible and pay attention to your body's normal rhythms to get the most out of your plant-based diet. You will also notice that I refer to taking meals to work. Of course, if you work at home (stay at home mom or if your office is in your home) modify accordingly.

**WEEK ONE: SUNDAY**

1. **Morning:** Make pumpkin muffins for breakfast, store remaining muffins in the freezer. While muffins are baking, make Almond Coconut Cranberry Bars and keep in the freezer.
2. **Lunch:** Make Lentil Cashew Dressing (reserve half of dressing in a glass container and store in the refrigerator).
3. **Either at lunch or late afternoon:** Make Apricot Beet Salad, divide in half and store in separate containers in the refrigerator. Make six walnut stuffed dates and store in the refrigerator.
4. **Dinner:** Make Asparagus Orange Quinoa. While quinoa is cooking, chop fruit of choice

(apples, berries) and store in refrigerator for Monday morning. Chop ripe bananas (3-5) into bite-sized pieces and place in plastic bag in freezer so you are always ready to make Nanacream when the need arises! Periodically through each week, freeze extra ripe bananas to continually replenish your supply.

## MONDAY

1. **Morning:** Take pre-cut fruit from the refrigerator, add nuts, seeds, and dried fruit.

2. **Take to work** container of reserved Apricot Beet Salad from refrigerator and one or two Almond Coconut Cranberry Bars from the freezer.

3. **Dinner:** Steam veggies of choice (broccoli, red or green peppers, squash). Drain and rinse one can of black beans, add 1/4 cup chopped red onion and mix in a small bowl. Reserve 1/4 cup in a container in the refrigerator. Add 1/2 chopped avocado and gently mix. Store the other avocado half in the refrigerator. Make Blueberry Nanacream for dessert if desired.

## TUESDAY

1. **Morning:** Make Green Smoothie (if you have extra, take to work for a snack or to have with lunch).

2. **Pack for work** container of black beans/onions, avocado, handful of carrots, bag of rice cakes (keep at your desk for snacking), apple or pear, 2 Walnut-stuffed Dates from refrigerator.

3. **Dinner:** Press tofu, cut veggies of choice, chop red onion (reserve 2 tbsp and set aside), and chop garlic. Use a box grater and grate 2 carrots, mix in 1/2 can garbanzo beans and reserved red onion, and store in a glass container in the refrigerator. Place other half of beans in separate container in the refrigerator. Make Tofu Scramble. While it is cooking, make Creamy Mustard Dressing (reserve 1/8 - 1/4 cup for Wednesday lunch).

4. **After dinner,** during kitchen clean up, make Dena's Power Nut/Seed Butter (12 minutes in the food processor). Reserve 2-3 tbsp in a small container to take for lunch on Wednesday (or if using store-bought nut butter, reserve 2-3 tbsp) and store the remainder in the refrigerator.

## WEDNESDAY

1. **Morning:** Make oatmeal, sprinkle with nuts and dried fruit.

2. **Pack for work** a small bowl for mixing, pre-prepared container of garbanzo, carrots, onion, leftover Creamy Mustard dressing, nut butter, apple, 2 slices whole grain bread.

3. **Lunch:** Empty garbanzo, carrots, onion in small mixing bowl and slightly mash garbanzo with a fork. Spread dressing on both slices of bread, add garbanzo spread.

4. **Dinner:** Make Carrot Curry Soup (reserve 1/2 cup for Thursday lunch). Make Avocado Mango Pistachio Dressing (reserve 1/4 cup for Thursday lunch). Place pre-washed spinach or other greens into a salad bowl, add chopped tomatoes, mushrooms, remaining garbanzo beans in the refrigerator and toss with dressing.

5. **Prepare for Thursday:** Pack reserved soup and dressing, small container of pre-washed spinach or other greens, 3 tbsp tahini in a container, small bag of cacao nibs, and a banana. Take pumpkin muffin from freezer and put in a covered container on countertop for Thursday breakfast.

## THURSDAY

1. **Morning:** Heat pumpkin muffin in microwave if desired.

2. **Take food items to work** that were set aside last night for today's lunch.

3. **Dinner:** Make Pinto Bean Basil Dip (reserve 1/4 cup for Friday lunch). Chop 1/2 cup each snow peas, red pepper, mushrooms, red onion and place in a steamer for 7-10 minutes (reserve 1/4 of the mixture for Friday lunch). Chop 2-3 carrots into thin matchsticks. Sauté cubed tempeh in a small amount of coconut oil, turning several times to brown multiple sides (reserve 1/4 of the tempeh for Friday lunch). While waiting for the tempeh to cook, wash and dry 3 large Romaine leaves. Store

in the refrigerator wrapped in paper towels in crisper bin for Friday's lunch. In a medium-sized bowl mix tempeh and steamed vegetables with Pinto Bean Basil Dip to lightly coat the mixture. Plate as is or on a bed of greens. Serve remaining dip with carrots on the side. Make nanacream (add berry or fruit of choice) or slice fruit in a bowl and top with sprinkled coconut and cacao nibs.

## FRIDAY

1. **Morning:** Add fruit to non-dairy yogurt.
2. **Take food items to work** that were set aside last night for today's lunch: Romaine leaves, a handful of pre-washed spinach, 2-3 rice cakes, and one avocado.
3. **Lunch:** Add to romaine wraps Pinto Bean Basil Dip, tempeh, and steamed vegetables.
4. **Dinner:** Take the night off and go out to dinner. Check your banana supply and chop in bite-sized pieces all ripe bananas and store in the freezer.

## SATURDAY

1. **Morning:** Make a Green Smoothie.
2. **Lunch:** Make Honeydew Cucumber Soup.
3. **Dinner:** Make Wheatberry Salad with Raisins (reserve 1/2 cup for Sunday lunch). While wheatberries are cooking for one hour, make Garbanzo Protein Chocolate Cookies.

## WEEK TWO: SUNDAY

1. **Morning:** Greens and Fruit Bowl.
2. **Make weekly shopping list, schedule grocery shopping today.**
3. **Lunch:** Wheatberry Salad with Raisins.
4. **Dinner:** Make Black Bean Enchiladas with Zucchini and Corn. (After cooking completed, reserve two enchiladas for lunch tomorrow and store in the refrigerator.)
5. **While enchiladas are baking,** make Cacao Chia Bars and place in freezer, then make Cilantro Pesto and store 1/4 cup in freezer and remainder in refrigerator. Put together six medjool dates stuffed with chopped walnuts and store in the refrigerator.

## MONDAY

1. **Morning:** Dairy-free yogurt with berries and nuts.
2. **Take food items to work** that were set aside last night for today's lunch: enchiladas, 1/4-1/2 cup granola, 1-2 kiwi, and an orange.
3. **Lunch:** Enchiladas (leftovers).
4. **Dinner:** Make Quinoa Salad with Cilantro Pesto (pre-made in refrigerator). After cooked, reserve 1/2 cup for Tuesday lunch and store in the refrigerator.

## TUESDAY

1. **Morning:** Make Millet with toppings of choice.
2. **Take food items to work** that were set aside last night for today's lunch: Quinoa, 2 carrots, 2 Walnut-stuffed Dates.
3. **Lunch:** Quinoa Salad with Cilantro Pesto (leftovers), side of carrots.
4. **Dinner:** Prepare a Lentil and Roasted or Steamed Veggie Dish (2 cups of veggies, add chopped onions and garlic). After cooked dish cools, reserve 1/2 cup (prior to mixing in dressing) and store in the refrigerator for Wednesday lunch. While dinner is cooking, make Asian Dressing (reserve 1/4 cup for Wednesday lunch), peel a Cantaloupe and slice it and store it in the refrigerator (reserving slices in a separate container for Wednesday lunch).

## WEDNESDAY

1. **Morning:** Fruit Smoothie of choice.
2. **Take food items to work** that were set aside last night for today's lunch: lentils and veggies, Asian dressing, coconut wraps, and cantaloupe slices.
3. **Lunch:** Coconut wraps with lentils, veggies, and Asian dressing.
4. **Dinner:** Make Traditional Hummus and reserve 1/2 cup for soup to be made on Thursday for dinner (store in refrigerator) and serve remaining hummus with crackers along with Dinner Salad.
5. **Prepare for Thursday:** Make Strawberry Hemp Dressing and reserve 1/4 cup for

breakfast on Thursday. Make Sesame Oil Cucumber Miso dish and store in refrigerator for Thursday lunch. Take Pumpkin Muffin from freezer and place in refrigerator to unthaw.

## THURSDAY

1. **Morning:** Prepare Greens and Fruit, use Strawberry Hemp Dressing.

2. **Take food items to work** that were set aside last night for today's lunch: Sesame Oil Cucumber Miso dish, Pumpkin Muffin, 1/4-1/2 cup granola, apple and berries.

3. **Lunch:** Sesame Oil Cucumber Miso dish with Granola mixed with chopped apple and berries.

4. **Dinner:** Make Cauliflower Quinoa Hummus Soup (use pre-made hummus stored in refrigerator). Reserve 1/2 cup of soup for Friday lunch. While soup is simmering, combine 1/2 cup black beans and 1/4 cup chopped red onion in a container in the refrigerator.

## FRIDAY

1. **Morning:** Make Green Smoothie.

2. **Take food items to work** that were set aside last night for today's lunch: Cauliflower Soup, black bean and onion mixture, 1 avocado, rice cakes, 1-2 Almond Coconut Cranberry Bars from the freezer.

3. **Lunch:** Heat up Cauliflower Soup, mix chopped avocado with black beans and onions and spread on rice cakes.

4. Dinner: Make Cabbage Carrot Cucumber Slaw first. Then make Roasted Broccoli w/ Tahini (short cooking time). Prepare Chorella Banana Bowl and refrigerate for Saturday breakfast.

## SATURDAY

1. **Morning:** Chorella Banana Bowl.

2. **Lunch:** Make Apricot Beet Salad.

3. **Dinner:** Take the night off and go out for a healthy dinner.

## WEEK THREE: SUNDAY

1. **Morning:** Oatmeal with toppings of choice.

2. **Make weekly shopping list, schedule grocery shopping today.**

3. **Lunch:** Apricot Beet Salad (leftovers).

4. **Make** Wheatgerm Flax w/Cranberry Muffins. **Make** Apricot Hemp Squares and store in the freezer.

5. **Dinner:** Make Ratatouille with Tofu (reserve 1/2 cup of dish for Monday lunch).

## WEEK THREE-WEEK FOUR

Now it's your turn to follow the templates I've provided and create your Prep Plan for Weeks Three and Four of the pre-designated menu. As you start out with this new lifestyle, practicing this Prep thought process will make sure you make healthy dishes that can also be eaten as leftovers the following day for lunch, maintain a supply of baked goods and bars in the freezer so they are always available when you need a snack, and if you work away from home during the week, ensure you think ahead to have extra plant-based foods (fruits, nuts, seeds, rice cakes etc.) available in addition to your pre-planned lunch.

Once you get the hang of this practice, whether you work outside of the home or inside your home, you won't need to be so regimented (writing directions out for each day) because it will come naturally for you to think about what you will take to work the following day for lunch and snacks, and to plan accordingly. It may take you one month, two months, or three months to get the hang of it, but stay with it because it is worth it and will actually remove one of your weekly stresses (and often guilt) of how to eat healthy dishes all day long, every day. Being organized is especially important if you are a stay-at-home mom because, as you know, your schedule will never be the same two days in a row!

Whenever making dressings or dips, always reserve about 1/4 cup directly after making it to use the following day in a wrap or on a salad, and do the same with soups. Otherwise, you might just eat the whole thing!

## Common Food Prep Technique Tips

**Determining when bananas are ripe and storage:** Bananas are fully ripe when the skin has small brown spots and the banana is soft to the touch. Buy bananas in bulk and allow them to ripen. Often, they ripen faster than we can eat them and since as plant-based gurus we don't waste food – peel the ripest bananas, chop into bite-sized pieces (never freeze the banana whole) and place in a resealable plastic bag in the freezer. If you keep up with this practice you will always have frozen bananas ready whenever you need them (it usually takes 4-5 hours, or better yet overnight, for bananas to completely freeze) to make nancream or throw into a smoothie. When you are ready to use the frozen banana, just remove the bag from the freezer and you will easily be able to break apart the bite-sized pieces and add to your Vitamix or blender.

**How to remove the rind and slice a melon:** Set the melon on a cutting board and with a long knife, trim off both ends. Stand the melon upright on one of the flat ends and start slicing the rind off the melon from top to bottom following the curve of the melon. Rotate the melon while you slice until all of the rind has been removed. Slice the melon in half and over a counter top garbage bowl, take a spoon and scrape out the seeds. Place each melon half on the cutting board and slice lengthwise (in rows). Place each piece flat side down, cut lengthwise again, then in cubes. Place in a glass container, cover and refrigerate.

**How to remove the skin and slice a papaya:** Use a vegetable peeler to remove the outer skin of the papaya. Slice the skinned papaya in half and over a counter top garbage bowl take a spoon and scrape out the seeds. Place each melon half on the cutting board and slice lengthwise (in rows), place each piece flat side down, cut lengthwise again, then in cubes. Place in a glass container, cover and refrigerate.

**How to slice and remove the pit from a mango:** Use a vegetable peeler to remove the outer skin of the mango. Set the mango on its end and notice its shape has two fat and two narrow sides. Locate the fatter side and place your paring knife just off center to avoid the pit and slice from top to bottom. Do the same on the other side of the pit, resulting in three large slices. Take the slice containing the pit and use your knife to remove remaining fruit on the two narrow sides next to the pit. Now make lengthwise slices on the other two remaining thirds and if you want cubes, cut each slice into cubes. Place in a glass container, cover and refrigerate.

**How to buy, store, and wash greens:** You will be increasing your consumption of greens, so in order to benefit from the nutrients greens provide you will want to consume them when they are the freshest which means they will be on your weekly shopping list. When you are at the market, choose those organic with the darkest green leaves and are crisp. Once you get home, remove the greens from plastic grocery bags (you can also purchase re-usable fabric produce bags to transport your greens from the grocery store to your refrigerator and cut back on the use of plastic bags) and place in a paper towel lined large glass or plastic container in one layer, don't overfill. Cover the greens with another paper towel(s) and place the cover on the container.

Store greens in the crisper portion of the refrigerator (or at least on the lowest shelf) where it is not as cold, preventing possible freezing of tender greens. Those that last the longest in the refrigerator include the sturdier greens: kale, romaine, and collard greens. Those that are more delicate: baby spinach, arugula, and spring mix may only last a day or two in the refrigerator so meal plan accordingly to minimize waste.

When you are ready to eat your greens, make sure to rinse well under water or fill the sink with water and soak greens briefly and then gently rinse. Whichever method you choose, always put clean greens in your salad spinner to remove as much excess water as possible. Transfer to a large salad bowl, add your mix-ins and dressings, and you're good to go!

One of the best ways to eat the more robust greens like kale and collards is to very finely chop them prior to adding them to your salad bowl. It really makes them much easier to eat and helps out in the first phase of digestion which is the mastication (chewing) and break down of food prior to reaching the stomach. If it is crunch you are looking for in your salads, make sure to add finely chopped cabbage (red or green) to other greens, mix them up and add a thick, substantial dressing.

**How to store herbs:** Herbs when purchased fresh can be prolonged by placing stem-trimmed herbs in a Mason jar half filled with water. Place the jar in the refrigerator and pull out herbs as needed for each recipe. Perfect for bunches of cilantro and parsley.

**How to peel fresh ginger:** Hold the ginger knob in your left hand, flip a spoon over, and hold it in your right hand, using the edge to scrape the outer layer off the ginger, scraping away from your body.

**Draining and Pressing Tofu:** Prepare tofu by draining off excess water. Remove tofu from the package and drain off any liquid. Place the tofu blocks on a plate with 2 layers of paper towels. Place a third paper towel on top of tofu and press lightly to remove initial water. Remove the top damp paper towel and replace with a new paper towel. Place cutting board on the towel and tofu. Place two cans (canned beans are ideal) on top of the cutting board and leave for 20 minutes. Remove cans, cutting board, and paper towels, transfer tofu blocks to a cutting board and cut into cubes or strips.

**How to open an avocado and cut bite-sized pieces of flesh:** Cut the avocado in half lengthwise following the outline of the pit. If the avocado is ripe, you should be able to twist apart the top and bottom pieces to expose the interior, and the pit should stay with one half. Use a spoon to scoop out the pit. (Some people use a knife to tap the pit so the knife's edge wedges into the pit, then twist the pit out of the avocado, but this takes practice, and you can easily cut your hand during this process.) Using a butter knife, make cuts in the avocado flesh in a cross-hatch pattern (bite-sized squares) without cutting through the avocado skin. Use a spoon and place it between the flesh and skin and carefully scoop out the bite-sized pieces.

**Plan on Leftovers:** Whenever making a dressing or dip, always reserve about 1/4-1/2 cup directly after making it to use the following day in a wrap or on a salad, and do the same with soups. Save a 1/2 cup and eat for lunch, pairing with a green salad.

## Concluding Remarks

At first it was difficult. It took me time to figure out all the ins and outs of the plant-based lifestyle. I also had to give my body a chance to adjust to the new foods, higher fiber content, and for me, weaning off of high animal-fat desserts. Once I became comfortable planning and preparing plant-based meals and found local vegan restaurants where I could eat out with my husband, everything became much easier. I also felt extraordinarily good about not compromising the livelihood of animals to sustain my nutritional needs.

I started to discover other people in my friendship ring or working in plant-based eateries that not only could relate to me but had noticed the changes in my energy levels, vibrancy, and fitness. My true realization of transition came when one of my close relatives told me I had a glow from the inside that was unmistakable. (She soon started adding healthy smoothies to her daily routine.) The only change I had made (besides getting older) was to adhere to veganism. The plant-based lifestyle soon became a passion that I wanted to share with everyone knowing it could improve their health and wellness, as well as protect animals and the environment. Simply, that is why I wrote this book.

I know you too will reap the benefits of this lifestyle if you give it a chance. Remember this can start at any level, from one meal a week, one meal a day, or working toward the full-blown plant-based life style at every meal. At whatever level you choose to commit to, as long as you plan ahead, organize, and prioritize how and what you eat, you will be successful. I hope this book provides you with encouragement, creative recipes, nutritional information, and fellow plant-based advocates that you need to jump start your life!

Made in the USA
San Bernardino, CA
09 October 2018